Collected Lyrics

Collected Lyrics

Collected Lyrics

of

Edna St. Vincent Millay

A Perennial Classic
Harper & Row, Publishers, New York

INTRODUCTION

When I was informed by Harper & Row, who have published the poetry of Edna St. Vincent Millay since 1923, that they wanted now to include her *Collected Lyrics* (as originally, and still, published by them) in their Perennial Library paperback series, I was delighted and agreed immediately. More than ever, it would seem, we need our poets, and their works should be made as accessible as possible. There have been few poets of our time as highly esteemed as Millay, and it is very probable that no modern poet has been so widely read. I am nevertheless aware that through the wide distribution of these editions many copies will come into the possession of readers who will have little acquaintance with the work or with the life of Edna St. Vincent Millay. Much of her poetry is contained in these volumes, and I have been asked to supply an outline of her life.

These collections were compiled by the poet and published in the early forties and could be said to embrace, with the most notable exceptions of her plays in poetry, her poetic works up to that time. She had wanted to include several poems from *Conversation at Midnight* which are complete in themselves, but decided against separating them from the *Conversation.* Her last volume of poetry, *Mine the Harvest,* said by many to contain some of her best work, was published posthumously in 1954.

When a poet publishes his work he wishes it to be known. If he wanted special and limited audiences he would have to bring out limited editions and distribute them among friends and admirers, or readers with credentials subject to the author's veto. It is my wish and hope that these books will go far and wide to refresh established followers and to establish new readers everywhere. The fact that this poet has always been widely read has brought her detractors. Karl Shapiro, poet and critic, in a critical review of Millay, said of this: "Poets have held her popularity against her for a generation. . . . They should read the collected lyrics and collected sonnets again. For Miss Millay was a poet of lyric genius. . . ." My further hope is, then, that these poems will be read freshly through the eyes and minds of you who approach them; that you will discover for yourselves what this poet has to say and that you will be receptive to the rich and subtle melodies in which she speaks.

A bronze plaque at 200 Broadway in Rockland, Maine, tells us that "Edna St. Vincent Millay, poet, was born in this house" and that the plaque was "Placed by The Woman's Educational Club, 1935." A further plan afoot at that time, by another Maine organization, to place signs up the coastal highway pointing the way to her birthplace, was quickly discouraged by that horrified lady. In 1968 a plaque was placed atop Mount Battie above Penobscot Bay in Camden Hills State Park where words from "Renascence," which speak of these mountains, the islands and the bay below, are imprinted in bronze. Here, we are told, "so deeply affected by her surroundings, she wrote 'Renascence' . . . the inspired beginning of the career of America's finest lyric poet."

From February 22, 1892, George Washington's birthday became rather, for her family and admirers, the birthday of a small, red-haired girl. Shortly after this date her parents moved inland to Union, where her father's people lived. Her two sisters were born here. Henry Millay became Superintendent of Schools and taught in the high school; Cora Millay found time for her music and writing; and this began as a happy family. When differences in attitude and ambition became established, a separation ended in divorce, and Mrs. Millay took on the care of her daughters herself. To support them she became a practical nurse, and moved her family to Rockport, back on the sea.

Her mother and her small Mason & Hamlin organ had opened for Vincent, as she was called from the first, the way to the world of music, and when the family moved to Newburyport, Massachusetts, where Mrs. Millay had spent her childhood, Vincent had the excitement of taking "real" piano lessons. She had been writing verses from a very early age, and poems she now entered in the "League" for young people in *St. Nicholas* magazine won recognition immediately; by the time she reached the age limit she had received all the honor badges offered for excellence and their top honor, the cash prize.

The Millays returned to Maine and settled in Camden as their permanent home. Camden is an exceptionally beautiful place in which to grow up. Where else on this coast do mountains rise so directly from the sea? And such friendly mountains, high enough to make one glad of a pause in which to look out over the bay, but possible to climb and get back in time for dinner. Vincent got to know Mount Battie and Mount Megunticook well and to know as well Penobscot Bay below them. It was a happy life, full of joy and full of interest. That money was scarce at times was simply part of it and to be expected, a contingency that bound this family close. There was music always; there was a room lined with books; there were three to play together, work together, picnic on the rocks. And there were the close, special friends.

Vincent was always keenly interested in anything she was doing. She was now in high school and she was a good student. As editor of the school magazine, *The Megunticook*, she wrote generously for it, poems and essays. At her graduation in 1909, she said her first long poem, "La Joie de Vivre," to a charmed audience —and was further gratified by receiving the prize of ten dollars. And here in high school her interest in theatre began. She acted in the plays, wrote a Halloween play for her class to present, branched out into local theatricals and even had the thrill of being engaged by a professional company for a brief out-of-town tour. Thus were her interests formed: poetry, music and the theatre.

Having finished her schooling, as far as she could know, there being certainly no finances for college and so no expressed thought of it, she continued, when her mother was on nursing cases, to keep house for her sisters still in school, to continue her music and to write and perfect her poems.

When she was nineteen, E. Vincent Millay, as she signed herself at this time, wrote a poem she called "Renascence," and in the following spring of 1912 entered it in *The Lyric Year* contest from which poems by one hundred American poets were to be chosen for inclusion in this volume. Her poem was accepted and she was elated, joyful. As revealed on publication in the fall, the editor's vote for the first prize of five hundred dollars was cast for "Renascence." The other two judges voted differently so it failed to receive a prize, a fact which caused more than a stir of indignation on the part of many critics and poets who greeted the appearance of this poem as an important literary event.

Nineteen twelve was a glowing year for her. Summer visitors to Camden, hearing her sing her songs and read her poems, became interested in arranging further education for her at college. Vincent chose Vassar. When, in 1913, she entered Barnard for a semester to make up necessary work, she was, perhaps, a unique student—in literary circles throughout the country she was already a poet known and admired. In New York, while living at the YWCA Training School, of which her benefactress was the head, she was introduced and feted, so to speak, by the literati. Vincent enjoyed college and got a great deal from it. At Vassar, in spite of the demands on time and energy and her stubborn refusal to curtail her writing, she still found time for college activities—to act in the plays and to produce her own plays for the college. She won song and poetry contests. The songs for Tree Ceremonies were hers and she wrote, at graduation in 1917, both words and music of the Baccalaureate Hymn.

Greenwich Village, the old quarter around Washington Square, offered a home and haven for young writers and artists because one could live there on very little money, which was usually what they had. It was what Vincent Millay had, just graduated from college, when she decided to stay in New York and look for work in the theatre. Her first book, *Renascence and Other Poems*, was published that year and was well received. Over the next three years she did many rewarding things: she joined the Provincetown Players group, acted in their plays and directed her own *Aria da Capo* and *The Princess Marries the Page* and acted with The Theatre Guild in their first production. And she had begun giving poetry readings. For a livelihood she wrote stories and articles for magazines under the pseudonym Nancy Boyd. But foremost always was her poetry.

How would her sister describe her? She was small—piquant perhaps is a good word. She was usually unusually beautiful, sustained in any mood by her bright and lively hair, called red but with gold and darker lights and suiting its natural waves to her delicate face and head. Saying her poems alone on a stage, she became tall with her friendly dignity. Her voice was extraordinary. Her eyes were green and looked both inward and out.

When, feeling the need of a change, Edna St. Vincent left for Europe and travel with an assignment from *Vanity Fair*, in the early winter of 1921, she had three books ready for publication—*Second April*, *Aria da Capo* and *A Few Figs from Thistles*, this last a gathering of her gayer and more cynical verses from over the years.

During her years in Europe, Millay lived in Paris, Rome, Vienna, Budapest; and made an exciting trip through the wild country of Albania on horseback. With her mother, who joined her in Europe, she settled for a time in the English countryside, from which she could make frequent trips to London. Cold weather sent them to the south of France, but travel and alien foods had undermined the poet's health and they returned to America early in 1923. Millay had written steadily while in Europe. *Second April* had been highly praised, and now *The Harp-Weaver and Other Poems* was published and received the Pulitzer Prize. Through care and surgery her health was restored.

This year the poet met and married Eugen Boissevain, a Dutch importer, and together in 1924 they took a leisurely trip around the world. They bought a place in the Berkshires and, in 1925, gave up their house in New York and moved to their house on a hilltop, surrounded by some eight hundred acres of rolling country and woods, which they named Steepletop (now designated by the State as a historic landmark). And this became their home to renovate and enjoy and to which to return after travel, after reading tours, after winters in New York, Florida, the Virgin Islands. Later they purchased a rugged island in Casco Bay, Maine, and midsummers found them there.

But Edna St. Vincent was a poet always, and wherever she was she wrote. Books appeared—*The Buck in the Snow; Wine from These Grapes; Fatal Interview; Conversation at Midnight; Flowers of Evil*, translations of the poems of Baudelaire, with George Dillon; and *Huntsman, What Quarry?* She wrote *The King's Henchman*, the book for an opera by Deems Taylor, produced at the Metropolitan Opera House. And Millay was also an excellent reader of poetry—a rare enough gift—and she did much to promote interest in this activity. Her cross-country readings of her poems were to crowded houses. Her Sunday night broadcasts were an innovation, placing poetry for the first time beside music as a radio feature. The Millay album of her poetry recordings, issued in 1941, is now available on an LP record under the Caedmon label TC 1123.

An accident in the late thirties resulted in an injury to her back, and it was after years of constant pain and search for relief and cure that a doctor was found who understood the nature of the injury and proceeded to correct it. During these sick and depleted years, World War II embroiled Europe and, beyond her concern and distress for England, France and the Low Countries, Millay saw the approaching danger to her own country, unprepared. To help alert the nation she wrote unceasingly. When the war came to America she continued writing—poems, radio plays, speeches, whatever was asked of her—until her strength finally gave out in a nervous breakdown.

It was a slow recovery, discouragingly so. But, after the war, her life again found the pattern of work, and this was sustaining. She and her husband again found delight in Steepletop and Ragged Island. Poems accumulated toward her new book. She grew strong.

Eugen Boissevain died in August, 1949. Vincent insisted upon staying alone at Steepletop, to attempt in her own way to adjust to life without him. The hired man came as usual each day to do the chores and what errands were needed, and during that stark winter she trained her mind to her work. Soon there would be a book. But she did not live to complete and compile it. Edna St. Vincent Millay died in the early morning of October 19, in 1950, after working through the night.

And, since this brief biography will precede her poetry here, I will bridge the life to the work by quoting from what the eminent critic Edmund Wilson has written of her in his *Shores of Light:* ". . . Edna St. Vincent Millay seems to me one of the only poets writing in English in our time who have attained to anything like the stature of great literary figures . . . she does have it in common with [Eliot, Auden, Yeats] . . . that, in giving supreme expression to profoundly felt personal experience, she was able to identify herself with more general experience and stand forth as a spokesman for the human spirit. . . ."

NORMA MILLAY

Steepletop, 1959, 1969

CONTENTS

From *Second April*

From *A Few Figs from Thistles*

From *The Harp-Weaver and Other Poems*

From *The Buck in the Snow*

From *Poems Selected for Young People*

From a Very Little Sphinx

From *Wine from These Grapes*

From *Huntsman, What Quarry?*

From *RENASCENCE*

Renascence

All I could see from where I stood
Was three long mountains and a wood;
I turned and looked another way,
And saw three islands in a bay.
So with my eyes I traced the line
Of the horizon, thin and fine,
Straight around till I was come
Back to where I'd started from;
And all I saw from where I stood
Was three long mountains and a wood.

Over these things I could not see:
These were the things that bounded me.
And I could touch them with my hand,
Almost, I thought, from where I stand!
And all at once things seemed so small
My breath came short, and scarce at all.

But, sure, the sky is big, I said:
Miles and miles above my head.
So here upon my back I'll lie
And look my fill into the sky.

And so I looked, and after all,
The sky was not so very tall.
The sky, I said, must somewhere stop . . .
And—sure enough!—I see the top!
The sky, I thought, is not so grand;
I 'most could touch it with my hand!
And reaching up my hand to try,
I screamed, to feel it touch the sky.

I screamed, and—lo!—Infinity
Came down and settled over me;
Forced back my scream into my chest;
Bent back my arm upon my breast;
And, pressing of the Undefined
The definition on my mind,
Held up before my eyes a glass
Through which my shrinking sight did pass
Until it seemed I must behold
Immensity made manifold;
Whispered to me a word whose sound
Deafened the air for worlds around,
And brought unmuffled to my ears
The gossiping of friendly spheres,
The creaking of the tented sky,
The ticking of Eternity.

I saw and heard, and knew at last
The How and Why of all things, past,
And present, and forevermore.
The Universe, cleft to the core,
Lay open to my probing sense,
That, sickening, I would fain pluck thence
But could not,—nay! but needs must suck
At the great wound, and could not pluck
My lips away till I had drawn
All venom out.—Ah, fearful pawn:
For my omniscience paid I toll
In infinite remorse of soul.

All sin was of my sinning, all
Atoning mine, and mine the gall
Of all regret. Mine was the weight
Of every brooded wrong, the hate
That stood behind each envious thrust,
Mine every greed, mine every lust.

And all the while, for every grief,
Each suffering, I craved relief
With individual desire;
Craved all in vain! And felt fierce fire
About a thousand people crawl;
Perished with each,—then mourned for all!

A man was starving in Capri;
He moved his eyes and looked at me;
I felt his gaze, I heard his moan,
And knew his hunger as my own.

I saw at sea a great fog bank
Between two ships that struck and sank;
A thousand screams the heavens smote;
And every scream tore through my throat.

No hurt I did not feel, no death
That was not mine; mine each last breath
That, crying, met an answering cry
From the compassion that was I.
All suffering mine, and mine its rod;
Mine, pity like the pity of God.

Ah, awful weight! Infinity
Pressed down upon the finite Me!
My anguished spirit, like a bird,
Beating against my lips I heard;
Yet lay the weight so close about
There was no room for it without.
And so beneath the weight lay I
And suffered death, but could not die.

Long had I lain thus, craving death,
When quietly the earth beneath
Gave way, and inch by inch, so great
At last had grown the crushing weight,
Into the earth I sank till I
Full six feet under ground did lie,
And sank no more,—there is no weight
Can follow here, however great.
From off my breast I felt it roll,
And as it went my tortured soul
Burst forth and fled in such a gust
That all about me swirled the dust.

Deep in the earth I rested now.
Cool is its hand upon the brow
And soft its breast beneath the head
Of one who is so gladly dead.
And all at once, and over all
The pitying rain began to fall;
I lay and heard each pattering hoof
Upon my lowly, thatchèd roof,
And seemed to love the sound far more
Than ever I had done before.
For rain it hath a friendly sound
To one who's six feet under ground;
And scarce the friendly voice or face,
A grave is such a quiet place.

The rain, I said, is kind to come
And speak to me in my new home.
I would I were alive again
To kiss the fingers of the rain,
To drink into my eyes the shine
Of every slanting silver line,
To catch the freshened, fragrant breeze
From drenched and dripping apple-trees.
For soon the shower will be done,
And then the broad face of the sun
Will laugh above the rain-soaked earth
Until the world with answering mirth
Shakes joyously, and each round drop
Rolls, twinkling, from its grass-blade top.

How can I bear it, buried here,
While overhead the sky grows clear
And blue again after the storm?
O, multi-colored, multi-form,
Belovèd beauty over me,
That I shall never, never see
Again! Spring-silver, autumn-gold,
That I shall never more behold!—
Sleeping your myriad magics through,
Close-sepulchred away from you!

O God, I cried, give me new birth,
And put me back upon the earth!
Upset each cloud's gigantic gourd
And let the heavy rain, down-poured
In one big torrent, set me free,
Washing my grave away from me!

I ceased; and through the breathless hush
That answered me, the far-off rush
Of herald wings came whispering
Like music down the vibrant string
Of my ascending prayer, and—crash!
Before the wild wind's whistling lash
The startled storm-clouds reared on high
And plunged in terror down the sky!
And the big rain in one black wave
Fell from the sky and struck my grave.

I know not how such things can be;
I only know there came to me
A fragrance such as never clings
To aught save happy living things;
A sound as of some joyous elf
Singing sweet songs to please himself,
And, through and over everything,
A sense of glad awakening.

The grass, a-tiptoe at my ear,
Whispering to me I could hear;
I felt the rain's cool finger-tips
Brushed tenderly across my lips,
Laid gently on my sealèd sight,
And all at once the heavy night
Fell from my eyes and I could see!—
A drenched and dripping apple-tree,
A last long line of silver rain,
A sky grown clear and blue again.
And as I looked a quickening gust
Of wind blew up to me and thrust
Into my face a miracle
Of orchard-breath, and with the smell,—
I know not how such things can be!—
I breathed my soul back into me.

Ah! Up then from the ground sprang I
And hailed the earth with such a cry
As is not heard save from a man
Who has been dead, and lives again.
About the trees my arms I wound;
Like one gone mad I hugged the ground;
I raised my quivering arms on high;
I laughed and laughed into the sky;

Till at my throat a strangling sob
Caught fiercely, and a great heart-throb
Sent instant tears into my eyes:
O God, I cried, no dark disguise
Can e'er hereafter hide from me
Thy radiant identity!
Thou canst not move across the grass
But my quick eyes will see Thee pass,
Nor speak, however silently,
But my hushed voice will answer Thee.
I know the path that tells Thy way
Through the cool eve of every day;
God, I can push the grass apart
And lay my finger on Thy heart!

The world stands out on either side
No wider than the heart is wide;
Above the world is stretched the sky,—
No higher than the soul is high.
The heart can push the sea and land
Farther away on either hand;
The soul can split the sky in two,
And let the face of God shine through.
But East and West will pinch the heart
That can not keep them pushed apart;
And he whose soul is flat—the sky
Will cave in on him by and by.

Interim

The room is full of you!—As I came in
And closed the door behind me, all at once
A something in the air, intangible,
Yet stiff with meaning, struck my senses sick!—

Sharp, unfamiliar odours have destroyed
Each other room's dear personality.
The heavy scent of damp, funeral flowers,—
The very essence, hush-distilled, of Death—
Has strangled that habitual breath of home
Whose expiration leaves all houses dead;
And wheresoe'er I look is hideous change.
Save here. Here 'twas as if a weed-choked gate
Had opened at my touch, and I had stepped
Into some long-forgot, enchanted, strange,
Sweet garden of a thousand years ago
And suddenly thought, "I have been here before!"

You are not here. I know that you are gone,
And will not ever enter here again.
And yet it seems to me, if I should speak,
Your silent step must wake across the hall;
If I should turn my head, that your sweet eyes
Would kiss me from the door.—So short a time
To teach my life its transposition to
This difficult and unaccustomed key!—

The room is as you left it; your last touch—
A thoughtless pressure, knowing not itself
As saintly—hallows now each simple thing;
Hallows and glorifies, and glows between
The dust's grey fingers like a shielded light.

There is your book, just as you laid it down,
Face to the table,—I cannot believe
That you are gone!—Just then it seemed to me
You must be here. I almost laughed to think
How like reality the dream had been;
Yet knew before I laughed, and so was still.
That book, outspread, just as you laid it down!
Perhaps you thought, "I wonder what comes next,
And whether this or this will be the end";
So rose, and left it, thinking to return.
Perhaps that chair, when you arose and passed
Out of the room, rocked silently a while
Ere it again was still. When you were gone
Forever from the room, perhaps that chair,
Stirred by your movement, rocked a little while,
Silently, to and fro . . .

And here are the last words your fingers wrote,
Scrawled in broad characters across a page
In this brown book I gave you. Here your hand,
Guiding your rapid pen, moved up and down.

Here with a looping knot you crossed a "t,"
And here another like it, just beyond
These two eccentric "e's." You were so small,
And wrote so brave a hand!

How strange it seems
That of all words these are the words you chose!
And yet a simple choice; you did not know
You would not write again. If you had known—
But then, it does not matter,—and indeed
If you had known there was so little time
You would have dropped your pen and come to me
And this page would be empty, and some phrase
Other than this would hold my wonder now.
Yet, since you could not know, and it befell
That these are the last words your fingers wrote,
There is a dignity some might not see
In this, "I picked the first sweet-pea today."
Today! Was there an opening bud beside it
You left until tomorrow?—O my love,
The things that withered,—and you came not back!
That day you filled this circle of my arms
That now is empty. (O my empty life!)
That day—that day you picked the first sweet-pea,—
And brought it in to show me! I recall
With terrible distinctness how the smell
Of your cool gardens drifted in with you.
I know, you held it up for me to see
And flushed because I looked not at the flower,
But at your face; and when behind my look

You saw such unmistakable intent
You laughed and brushed your flower against my lips.
(You were the fairest thing God ever made,
I think.) And then your hands above my heart
Drew down its stem into a fastening,
And while your head was bent I kissed your hair.
I wonder if you knew. (Belovèd hands!
Somehow I cannot seem to see them still.
Somehow I cannot seem to see the dust
In your bright hair.) What is the need of Heaven
When earth can be so sweet?—If only God
Had let us love,—and show the world the way!
Strange cancellings must ink the eternal books
When love-crossed-out will bring the answer right!

That first sweet-pea! I wonder where it is.
It seems to me I laid it down somewhere,
And yet,—I am not sure. I am not sure,
Even, if it was white or pink; for then
'Twas much like any other flower to me,
Save that it was the first. I did not know,
Then, that it was the last. If I had known—
But then, it does not matter. Strange how few,
After all's said and done, the things that are
Of moment.

Few indeed! When I can make
Of ten small words a rope to hang the world!
"I had you and I have you now no more."
There, there it dangles,—where's the little truth
That can for long keep footing under that
When its slack syllables tighten to a thought?
Here, let me write it down! I wish to see
Just how a thing like that will look on paper!

"I had you and I have you now no more."

O little words, how can you run so straight
Across the page, beneath the weight you bear?
How can you fall apart, whom such a theme
Has bound together, and hereafter aid
In trivial expression, that have been
So hideously dignified?

Would God
That tearing you apart would tear the thread
I strung you on! Would God—O God, my mind
Stretches asunder on this merciless rack
Of imagery! Oh, let me sleep a while!
Would I could sleep, and wake to find me back
In that sweet summer afternoon with you.
Summer? 'Tis summer still by the calendar!
How easily could God, if He so willed,
Set back the world a little turn or two!—
Correct its griefs, and bring its joys again!

We were so wholly one I had not thought
That we could die apart. I had not thought

That I could move,—and you be stiff and still!
That I could speak,—and you perforce be dumb!
I think our heart-strings were, like warp and woof
In some firm fabric, woven in and out;
Your golden filaments in fair design
Across my duller fibre. And today
The shining strip is rent; the exquisite
Fine pattern is destroyed; part of your heart
Aches in my breast; part of my heart lies chilled
In the damp earth with you. I have been torn
In two, and suffer for the rest of me.
What is my life to me? And what am I
To life,—a ship whose star has guttered out?
A Fear that in the deep night starts awake
Perpetually, to find its senses strained
Against the taut strings of the quivering air,
Awaiting the return of some dread chord?

Dark, Dark, is all I find for metaphor;
All else were contrast;—save that contrast's wall
Is down, and all opposed things flow together
Into a vast monotony, where night
And day, and frost and thaw, and death and life,
Are synonyms. What now—what now to me
Are all the jabbering birds and foolish flowers
That clutter up the world? You were my song!
Now, now, let discord scream! You were my flower!
Now let the world grow weeds! For I shall not
Plant things above your grave—(the common balm
Of the conventional woe for its own wound!)

Amid sensations rendered negative
By your elimination stands today,
Certain, unmixed, the element of grief;
I sorrow; and I shall not mock my truth
With travesties of suffering, nor seek
To effigy its incorporeal bulk
In little wry-faced images of woe.
I cannot call you back; and I desire
No utterance of my immaterial voice.
I cannot even turn my face this way
Or that, and say, "My face is turned to you";
I know not where you are, I do not know
If heaven hold you or if earth transmute,
Body and soul, you into earth again;
But this I know:—not for one second's space
Shall I insult my sight with visionings
Such as the credulous crowd so eager-eyed
Beholds, self-conjured in the empty air.
Let the world wail! Let drip its easy tears!
My sorrow shall be dumb!

                —What do I say?
God! God!—God pity me! Am I gone mad
That I should spit upon a rosary?
Am I become so shrunken? Would to God
I too might feel that frenzied faith whose touch
Makes temporal the most enduring grief;
Though it must walk a while, as is its wont,
With wild lamenting! Would I too might weep

Where weeps the world and hangs its piteous wreaths
For its new dead! Not Truth, but Faith, it is
That keeps the world alive. If all at once
Faith were to slacken,—that unconscious faith
Which must, I know, yet be the corner-stone
Of all believing,—birds now flying fearless
Across, would drop in terror to the earth;
Fishes would drown; and the all-governing reins
Would tangle in the frantic hands of God
And the worlds gallop headlong to destruction!

O God, I see it now, and my sick brain
Staggers and swoons! How often over me
Flashes this breathlessness of sudden sight
In which I see the universe unrolled
Before me like a scroll and read thereon
Chaos and Doom, where helpless planets whirl
Dizzily round and round and round and round,
Like tops across a table, gathering speed
With every spin, to waver on the edge
One instant—looking over—and the next
To shudder and lurch forward out of sight!

Ah, I am worn out—I am wearied out—
It is too much—I am but flesh and blood,
And I must sleep. Though you were dead again,
I am but flesh and blood and I must sleep.

The Suicide

"Curse thee, Life, I will live with thee no more!
Thou hast mocked me, starved me, beat my body
    sore!
And all for a pledge that was not pledged by me,
I have kissed thy crust and eaten sparingly
That I might eat again, and met thy sneers
With deprecations, and thy blows with tears,—
Aye, from thy glutted lash, glad, crawled away,
As if spent passion were a holiday!
And now I go. Nor threat, nor easy vow
Of tardy kindness can avail thee now
With me, whence fear and faith alike are flown;
Lonely I came, and I depart alone,
And know not where nor unto whom I go;
But that thou canst not follow me I know."

Thus I to Life, and ceased; but through my brain
My thought ran still, until I spake again:

"Ah, but I go not as I came,—no trace
Is mine to bear away of that old grace
I brought! I have been heated in thy fires,
Bent by thy hands, fashioned to thy desires,
Thy mark is on me! I am not the same
Nor ever more shall be, as when I came.
Ashes am I of all that once I seemed.
In me all's sunk that leapt, and all that dreamed

Is wakeful for alarm,—oh, shame to thee,
For the ill change that thou hast wrought in me
Who laugh no more nor lift my throat to sing!
Ah, Life, I would have been a pleasant thing
To have about the house when I was grown
If thou hadst left my little joys alone!
I asked of thee no favour save this one:
That thou wouldst leave me playing in the sun!
And this thou didst deny, calling my name
Insistently, until I rose and came.
I saw the sun no more.—It were not well
So long on these unpleasant thoughts to dwell,
Need I arise tomorrow and renew
Again my hated tasks, but I am through
With all things save my thoughts and this one night;
So that in truth I seem already quite
Free and remote from thee,—I feel no haste
And no reluctance to depart; I taste
Merely, with thoughtful mien, an unknown draught,
That in a little while I shall have quaffed."

Thus I to Life, and ceased, and slightly smiled,
Looking at nothing; and my thin dreams filed
Before me one by one till once again
I set new words unto an old refrain:

"Treasures thou hast that never have been mine!
Warm lights in many a secret chamber shine
Of thy gaunt house, and gusts of song have blown
Like blossoms out to me that sat alone!

And I have waited well for thee to show
If any share were mine,—and now I go!
Nothing I leave, and if I naught attain
I shall but come into mine own again!"

Thus I to Life, and ceased, and spake no more,
But turning, straightway sought a certain door
In the rear wall. Heavy it was, and low
And dark,—a way by which none e'er would go
That other exit had, and never knock
Was heard thereat,—bearing a curious lock,
Some chance had shown me fashioned faultily,
Whereof Life held content the useless key;
And great coarse hinges, thick and rough with rust,
Whose sudden voice across a silence must,
I knew, be harsh and horrible to hear,—
A strange door, ugly like a dwarf.—So near
I came I felt upon my feet the chill
Of acid wind creeping across the sill.
So stood longtime, till over me at last
Came weariness, and all things other passed
To make it room; the still night drifted deep
Like snow about me, and I longed for sleep.

But, suddenly, marking the morning hour,
Bayed the deep-throated bell within the tower!
Startled, I raised my head,—and with a shout
Laid hold upon the latch,—and was without.

————————

Ah, long-forgotten, well-remembered road,
Leading me back unto my old abode,
My Father's house! There in the night I came,
And found them feasting, and all things the same
As they had been before. A splendour hung
Upon the walls, and such sweet songs were sung
As, echoing out of very long ago,
Had called me from the house of Life, I know.
So fair their raiment shone I looked in shame
On the unlovely garb in which I came;
Then straightway at my hesitancy mocked:
"It is my Father's house!" I said and knocked;
And the door opened. To the shining crowd
Tattered and dark I entered, like a cloud,
Seeing no face but His; to Him I crept,
And "Father!" I cried, and clasped His knees, and
    wept.

————

Ah, days of joy that followed! All alone
I wandered through the house. My own, my own,
My own to touch, my own to taste and smell,
All I had lacked so long and loved so well!
None shook me out of sleep, nor hushed my song,
Nor called me in from the sunlight all day long.

I know not when the wonder came to me
Of what my Father's business might be,
And whither fared and on what errands bent
The tall and gracious messengers He sent.

Yet one day with no song from dawn till night
Wondering, I sat, and watched them out of sight.
And the next day I called; and on the third
Asked them if I might go,—but no one heard.
Then, sick with longing, I arose at last
And went unto my Father,—in that vast
Chamber wherein He for so many years
Has sat, surrounded by His charts and spheres.
"Father," I said, "Father, I cannot play
The harp that Thou didst give me, and all day
I sit in idleness, while to and fro
About me Thy serene, grave servants go;
And I am weary of my lonely ease.
Better a perilous journey overseas
Away from Thee, than this, the life I lead,
To sit all day in the sunshine like a weed
That grows to naught,—I love Thee more than they
Who serve Thee most; yet serve Thee in no way.
Father, I beg of Thee a little task
To dignify my days,—'tis all I ask
Forever, but forever, this denied,
I perish."

      "Child," my Father's voice replied,
"All things thy fancy hath desired of me
Thou hast received. I have prepared for thee
Within my house a spacious chamber, where
Are delicate things to handle and to wear,
And all these things are thine. Dost thou love song?
My minstrels shall attend thee all day long.

24

Or sigh for flowers? My fairest gardens stand
Open as fields to thee on every hand.
And all thy days this word shall hold the same:
No pleasure shalt thou lack that thou shalt name.
But as for tasks—" He smiled, and shook His head;
"Thou hadst thy task, and laidst it by," He said.

God's World

O World, I cannot hold thee close enough!
   Thy winds, thy wide grey skies!
   Thy mists, that roll and rise!
Thy woods, this autumn day, that ache and sag
And all but cry with colour! That gaunt crag
To crush! To lift the lean of that black bluff!
World, World, I cannot get thee close enough!

Long have I known a glory in it all,
     But never knew I this:
     Here such a passion is
As stretcheth me apart,—Lord, I do fear
Thou'st made the world too beautiful this year;
My soul is all but out of me,—let fall
No burning leaf; prithee, let no bird call.

Afternoon on a Hill

I will be the gladdest thing
    Under the sun!
I will touch a hundred flowers
    And not pick one.

I will look at cliffs and clouds
    With quiet eyes,
Watch the wind bow down the grass,
    And the grass rise.

And when lights begin to show
    Up from the town,
I will mark which must be mine,
    And then start down!

Sorrow

Sorrow like a ceaseless rain
    Beats upon my heart.
People twist and scream in pain,—
Dawn will find them still again;
This has neither wax nor wane,
    Neither stop nor start.

People dress and go to town;
    I sit in my chair.
All my thoughts are slow and brown:
Standing up or sitting down
Little matters, or what gown
    Or what shoes I wear.

Tavern

I'll keep a little tavern
    Below the high hill's crest,
Wherein all grey-eyed people
    May sit them down and rest.

There shall be plates a-plenty,
    And mugs to melt the chill
Of all the grey-eyed people
    Who happen up the hill.

There sound will sleep the traveller,
    And dream his journey's end,
But I will rouse at midnight
    The falling fire to tend.

Aye, 'tis a curious fancy—
    But all the good I know
Was taught me out of two grey eyes
    A long time ago.

Ashes of Life

Love has gone and left me and the days are all alike;
  Eat I must, and sleep I will,—and would that night
    were here!
But ah!—to lie awake and hear the slow hours strike!
  Would that it were day again!—with twilight near!

Love has gone and left me and I don't know what
    to do;
  This or that or what you will is all the same to me;
But all the things that I begin I leave before I'm
    through,—
  There's little use in anything as far as I can see.

Love has gone and left me,—and the neighbours knock
    and borrow,
  And life goes on forever like the gnawing of a
    mouse,—
And tomorrow and tomorrow and tomorrow and
    tomorrow
  There's this little street and this little house.

The Little Ghost

I knew her for a little ghost
   That in my garden walked;
The wall is high—higher than most—
   And the green gate was locked.

And yet I did not think of that
   Till after she was gone—
I knew her by the broad white hat,
   All ruffled, she had on,

By the dear ruffles round her feet,
   By her small hands that hung
In their lace mitts, austere and sweet,
   Her gown's white folds among.

I watched to see if she would stay,
   What she would do—and oh!
She looked as if she liked the way
   I let my garden grow!

She bent above my favourite mint
   With conscious garden grace,
She smiled and smiled—there was no hint
   Of sadness in her face.

She held her gown on either side
  To let her slippers show,
And up the walk she went with pride,
  The way great ladies go.

And where the wall is built in new,
  And is of ivy bare,
She paused—then opened and passed through
  A gate that once was there.

Kin to Sorrow

Am I kin to Sorrow,
  That so oft
Falls the knocker of my door—
  Neither loud nor soft,
But as long accustomed—
  Under Sorrow's hand?
Marigolds around the step
  And rosemary stand,
And then comes Sorrow—
  And what does Sorrow care
For the rosemary
  Or the marigolds there?
Am I kin to Sorrow?
  Are we kin?
That so oft upon my door—
  Oh, come in!

Three Songs of Shattering

I

The first rose on my rose-tree
    Budded, bloomed, and shattered,
During sad days when to me
    Nothing mattered.

Grief of grief has drained me clean;
    Still it seems a pity
No one saw,—it must have been
    Very pretty.

II

Let the little birds sing;
    Let the little lambs play;
Spring is here; and so 'tis spring;—
    But not in the old way!

I recall a place
    Where a plum-tree grew;
There you lifted up your face,
    And blossoms covered you.

If the little birds sing,
    And the little lambs play,
Spring is here; and so 'tis spring—
    But not in the old way!

All the dog-wood blossoms are underneath the tree!
  Ere spring was going—ah, spring is gone!
And there comes no summer to the like of you and
    me,—
  Blossom time is early, but no fruit sets on.

All the dog-wood blossoms are underneath the tree,
  Browned at the edges, turned in a day;
And I would with all my heart they trimmed a mound
    for me,
  And weeds were tall on all the paths that led that
    way!

The Shroud

Death, I say, my heart is bowed
  Unto thine,—O mother!
This red gown will make a shroud
  Good as any other!

(I, that would not wait to wear
  My own bridal things,
In a dress dark as my hair
  Made my answerings.

I, to-night, that till he came
    Could not, could not wait,
In a gown as bright as flame
    Held for them the gate.)

Death, I say, my heart is bowed
    Unto thine,—O mother!
This red gown will make a shroud
    Good as any other!

The Dream

Love, if I weep it will not matter,
    And if you laugh I shall not care;
Foolish am I to think about it,
    But it is good to feel you there.

Love, in my sleep I dreamed of waking,—
    White and awful the moonlight reached
Over the floor, and somewhere, somewhere
    There was a shutter loose,—it screeched!—

Swung in the wind!—and no wind blowing!—
   I was afraid, and turned to you,
Put out my hand to you for comfort,—
   And you were gone! Cold, cold as dew,

Under my hand the moonlight lay!
   Love, if you laugh I shall not care,
But if I weep it will not matter,—
   Ah, it is good to feel you there!

Indifference

I said,—for Love was laggard, oh, Love was slow to
    come,—
   "I'll hear his step and know his step when I am
    warm in bed;
But I'll never leave my pillow, though there be some
   As would let him in—and take him in with tears!"
    I said.

I lay,—for Love was laggard, oh, he came not until
    dawn,—
   I lay and listened for his step and could not get to
    sleep;
And he found me at my window with my big cloak
    on,
   All sorry with the tears some folks might weep!

Witch-Wife

She is neither pink nor pale,
  And she never will be all mine;
She learned her hands in a fairy-tale,
  And her mouth on a valentine.

She has more hair than she needs;
  In the sun 'tis a woe to me!
And her voice is a string of coloured beads,
  Or steps leading into the sea.

She loves me all that she can,
  And her ways to my ways resign;
But she was not made for any man,
  And she never will be all mine.

Blight

Hard seeds of hate I planted
  That should by now be grown,—
Rough stalks, and from thick stamens
  A poisonous pollen blown,
And odours rank, unbreathable,
  From dark corollas thrown!

At dawn from my damp garden
  I shook the chilly dew;
The thin boughs locked behind me
  That sprang to let me through;
The blossoms slept,—I sought a place
  Where nothing lovely grew.

And there, when day was breaking,
  I knelt and looked around:
The light was near, the silence
  Was palpitant with sound;
I drew my hate from out my breast
  And thrust it in the ground.

Oh, ye so fiercely tended,
  Ye little seeds of hate!
I bent above your growing
  Early and noon and late,
Yet are ye drooped and pitiful,—
  I cannot rear ye straight!

The sun seeks out my garden,
  No nook is left in shade,
No mist nor mold nor mildew
  Endures on any blade,
Sweet rain slants under every bough:
  Ye falter, and ye fade.

When the Year Grows Old

I cannot but remember
  When the year grows old—
October—November—
  How she disliked the cold!

She used to watch the swallows
  Go down across the sky,
And turn from the window
  With a little sharp sigh.

And often when the brown leaves
  Were brittle on the ground,
And the wind in the chimney
  Made a melancholy sound,

She had a look about her
  That I wish I could forget—
The look of a scared thing
  Sitting in a net!

Oh, beautiful at nightfall
  The soft spitting snow!
And beautiful the bare boughs
  Rubbing to and fro!

But the roaring of the fire,
  And the warmth of fur,
And the boiling of the kettle
  Were beautiful to her!

I cannot but remember
  When the year grows old—
October—November—
  How she disliked the cold!

From *SECOND APRIL*

Spring

To what purpose, April, do you return again?
Beauty is not enough.
You can no longer quiet me with the redness
Of little leaves opening stickily.
I know what I know.
The sun is hot on my neck as I observe
The spikes of the crocus.
The smell of the earth is good.
It is apparent that there is no death.
But what does that signify?
Not only under ground are the brains of men
Eaten by maggots.
Life in itself
Is nothing,
An empty cup, a flight of uncarpeted stairs.
It is not enough that yearly, down this hill,
April
Comes like an idiot, babbling and strewing flowers.

City Trees

The trees along this city street,
    Save for the traffic and the trains,
Would make a sound as thin and sweet
    As trees in country lanes.

And people standing in their shade
  Out of a shower, undoubtedly
Would hear such music as is made
  Upon a country tree.

Oh, little leaves that are so dumb
  Against the shrieking city air,
I watch you when the wind has come,—
  I know what sound is there.

The Blue-Flag in the Bog

God had called us, and we came;
  Our loved Earth to ashes left;
Heaven was a neighbour's house,
  Open flung to us, bereft.

Gay the lights of Heaven showed,
  And 'twas God who walked ahead;
Yet I wept along the road,
  Wanting my own house instead.

Wept unseen, unheeded cried,
  "All you things my eyes have kissed,
Fare you well! We meet no more,
  Lovely, lovely tattered mist!

Weary wings that rise and fall
  All day long above the fire!"
(Red with heat was every wall,
  Rough with heat was every wire)

"Fare you well, you little winds
  That the flying embers chase!
Fare you well, you shuddering day,
  With your hands before your face!

And, ah, blackened by strange blight,
  Or to a false sun unfurled,
Now forevermore goodbye,
  All the gardens in the world!

On the windless hills of Heaven,
  That I have no wish to see,
White, eternal lilies stand,
  By a lake of ebony.

But the Earth forevermore
  Is a place where nothing grows,—
Dawn will come, and no bud break;
  Evening, and no blossom close.

Spring will come, and wander slow
   Over an indifferent land,
Stand beside an empty creek,
   Hold a dead seed in her hand."

———————

God had called us, and we came,
   But the blessèd road I trod
Was a bitter road to me,
   And at heart I questioned God.

"Though in Heaven," I said, "be all
   That the heart would most desire,
Held Earth naught save souls of sinners
   Worth the saving from a fire?

Withered grass,—the wasted growing!
   Aimless ache of laden boughs!"
Little things God had forgotten
   Called me, from my burning house.

"Though in Heaven," I said, "be all
   That the eye could ask to see,
All the things I ever knew
   Are this blaze in back of me."

"Though in Heaven," I said, "be all
    That the ear could think to lack,
All the things I ever knew
    Are this roaring at my back."

It was God who walked ahead,
    Like a shepherd to the fold;
In his footsteps fared the weak,
    And the weary and the old,

Glad enough of gladness over,
    Ready for the peace to be,—
But a thing God had forgotten
    Was the growing bones of me.

And I drew a bit apart,
    And I lagged a bit behind,
And I thought on Peace Eternal,
    Lest He look into my mind:

And I gazed upon the sky,
    And I thought of Heavenly Rest,—
And I slipped away like water
    Through the fingers of the blest!

All their eyes were fixed on Glory,
    Not a glance brushed over me;
"Alleluia! Alleluia!"
    Up the road,—and I was free.

And my heart rose like a freshet,
    And it swept me on before,
Giddy as a whirling stick,
    Till I felt the earth once more.

———————

All the Earth was charred and black,
    Fire had swept from pole to pole;
And the bottom of the sea
    Was as brittle as a bowl;

And the timbered mountain-top
    Was as naked as a skull,—
Nothing left, nothing left,
    Of the Earth so beautiful!

"Earth," I said, "how can I leave you?"
    "You are all I have," I said;
"What is left to take my mind up,
    Living always, and you dead?"

"Speak!" I said, "Oh, tell me something!
    Make a sign that I can see!
For a keepsake! To keep always!
    Quick!—before God misses me!"

And I listened for a voice;—
    But my heart was all I heard;
Not a screech-owl, not a loon,
    Not a tree-toad said a word.

And I waited for a sign;—
    Coals and cinders, nothing more;
And a little cloud of smoke
    Floating on a valley floor.

And I peered into the smoke
    Till it rotted, like a fog:—
There, encompassed round by fire,
    Stood a blue-flag in a bog!

Little flames came wading out,
    Straining, straining towards its stem,
But it was so blue and tall
    That it scorned to think of them!

Red and thirsty were their tongues,
  As the tongues of wolves must be,
But it was so blue and tall—
  Oh, I laughed, I cried, to see!

All my heart became a tear,
  All my soul became a tower,
Never loved I anything
  As I loved that tall blue flower!

It was all the little boats
  That had ever sailed the sea,
It was all the little books
  That had gone to school with me;

On its roots like iron claws
  Rearing up so blue and tall,—
It was all the gallant Earth
  With its back against a wall!

In a breath, ere I had breathed,—
  Oh, I laughed, I cried, to see!—
I was kneeling at its side,
  And it leaned its head on me!

———————

Crumbling stones and sliding sand
  Is the road to Heaven now;
Icy at my straining knees
  Drags the awful under-tow;

Soon but stepping-stones of dust
  Will the road to Heaven be,—
Father, Son and Holy Ghost,
  Reach a hand and rescue me!

"There—there, my blue-flag flower;
  Hush—hush—go to sleep;
That is only God you hear,
  Counting up His folded sheep!

Lullabye—lullabye—
  That is only God that calls,
Missing me, seeking me,
  Ere the road to nothing falls!

He will set His mighty feet
  Firmly on the sliding sand;
Like a little frightened bird
  I will creep into His hand;

I will tell Him all my grief,
   I will tell Him all my sin;
He will give me half His robe
   For a cloak to wrap you in.

Lullabye—lullabye—"
   Rocks the burnt-out planet free!—
Father, Son and Holy Ghost,
   Reach a hand and rescue me!

———————

Ah, the voice of love at last!
   Lo, at last the face of light!
And the whole of His white robe
   For a cloak against the night!

And upon my heart asleep
   All the things I ever knew!—
"Holds Heaven not some cranny, Lord,
   For a flower so tall and blue?"

All's well and all's well!
   Gay the lights of Heaven show!
In some moist and Heavenly place
   We will set it out to grow.

Journey

Ah, could I lay me down in this long grass
And close my eyes, and let the quiet wind
Blow over me—I am so tired, so tired
Of passing pleasant places! All my life,
Following Care along the dusty road,
Have I looked back at loveliness and sighed;
Yet at my hand an unrelenting hand
Tugged ever, and I passed. All my life long
Over my shoulder have I looked at peace;
And now I fain would lie in this long grass
And close my eyes.

       Yet onward!

                Cat-birds call
Through the long afternoon, and creeks at dusk
Are guttural. Whip-poor-wills wake and cry,
Drawing the twilight close about their throats.
Only my heart makes answer. Eager vines
Go up the rocks and wait; flushed apple-trees
Pause in their dance and break the ring for me;
Dim, shady wood-roads, redolent of fern
And bayberry, that through sweet bevies thread
Of round-faced roses, pink and petulant,
Look back and beckon ere they disappear.
Only my heart, only my heart responds.

Yet, ah, my path is sweet on either side
All through the dragging day,—sharp underfoot
And hot, and like dead mist the dry dust hangs—
But far, oh, far as passionate eye can reach,
And long, ah, long as rapturous eye can cling,
The world is mine: blue hill, still silver lake,
Broad field, bright flower, and the long white road;
A gateless garden, and an open path;
My feet to follow, and my heart to hold.

Eel-Grass

No matter what I say,
    All that I really love
Is the rain that flattens on the bay,
    And the eel-grass in the cove;
The jingle-shells that lie and bleach
    At the tide-line, and the trace
Of higher tides along the beach:
    Nothing in this place.

Elegy Before Death

There will be rose and rhododendron
   When you are dead and under ground;
Still will be heard from white syringas
   Heavy with bees, a sunny sound;

Still will the tamaracks be raining
   After the rain has ceased, and still
Will there be robins in the stubble,
   Grey sheep upon the warm green hill.

Spring will not ail nor autumn falter;
   Nothing will know that you are gone,—
Saving alone some sullen plough-land
   None but yourself sets foot upon;

Saving the may-weed and the pig-weed
   Nothing will know that you are dead,—
These, and perhaps a useless wagon
   Standing beside some tumbled shed.

Oh, there will pass with your great passing
   Little of beauty not your own,—
Only the light from common water,
   Only the grace from simple stone!

The Bean-Stalk

Ho, Giant! This is I!
I have built me a bean-stalk into your sky!
La,—but it's lovely, up so high!

This is how I came,—I put
Here my knee, there my foot,
Up and up, from shoot to shoot—
And the blessèd bean-stalk thinning
Like the mischief all the time,
Till it took me rocking, spinning,
In a dizzy, sunny circle,
Making angles with the root,
Far and out above the cackle
Of the city I was born in,
Till the little dirty city
In the light so sheer and sunny
Shone as dazzling bright and pretty
As the money that you find
In a dream of finding money—
What a wind! What a morning!—

Till the tiny, shiny city,
When I shot a glance below,
Shaken with a giddy laughter,
Sick and blissfully afraid,
Was a dew-drop on a blade,

And a pair of moments after
Was the whirling guess I made,—
And the wind was like a whip
Cracking past my icy ears,
And my hair stood out behind,
And my eyes were full of tears,
Wide-open and cold,
More tears than they could hold,
The wind was blowing so,
And my teeth were in a row,
Dry and grinning,
And I felt my foot slip,
And I scratched the wind and whined,
And I clutched the stalk and jabbered,
With my eyes shut blind,—
What a wind! What a wind!

Your broad sky, Giant,
Is the shelf of a cupboard;
I make bean-stalks, I'm
A builder, like yourself,
But bean-stalks is my trade,
I couldn't make a shelf,
Don't know how they're made,
Now, a bean-stalk is more pliant—
La, what a climb!

Weeds

White with daisies and red with sorrel
  And empty, empty under the sky!—
Life is a quest and love a quarrel—
  Here is a place for me to lie.

Daisies spring from damnèd seeds,
  And this red fire that here I see
Is a worthless crop of crimson weeds,
  Cursed by farmers thriftily.

But here, unhated for an hour,
  The sorrel runs in ragged flame,
The daisy stands, a bastard flower,
  Like flowers that bear an honest name.

And here a while, where no wind brings
  The baying of a pack athirst,
May sleep the sleep of blessèd things,
  The blood too bright, the brow accurst.

Passer Mortuus Est

Death devours all lovely things:
  Lesbia with her sparrow
Shares the darkness,—presently
  Every bed is narrow.

Unremembered as old rain
    Dries the sheer libation;
And the little petulant hand
    Is an annotation.

After all, my erstwhile dear,
    My no longer cherished,
Need we say it was not love,
    Just because it perished?

Pastoral

If it were only still!—
With far away the shrill
Crying of a cock;
Or the shaken bell
From a cow's throat
Moving through the bushes;
Or the soft shock
Of wizened apples falling
From an old tree
In a forgotten orchard
Upon the hilly rock!

Oh, grey hill,
Where the grazing herd
Licks the purple blossom,
Crops the spiky weed!
Oh, stony pasture,
Where the tall mullein
Stands up so sturdy
On its little seed!

Assault

I had forgotten how the frogs must sound
After a year of silence, else I think
I should not so have ventured forth alone
At dusk upon this unfrequented road.

I am waylaid by Beauty. Who will walk
Between me and the crying of the frogs?
Oh, savage Beauty, suffer me to pass,
That am a timid woman, on her way
From one house to another!

Travel

The railroad track is miles away,
  And the day is loud with voices speaking,
Yet there isn't a train goes by all day
  But I hear its whistle shrieking.

All night there isn't a train goes by,
  Though the night is still for sleep and dreaming,
But I see its cinders red on the sky,
  And hear its engine steaming.

My heart is warm with the friends I make,
  And better friends I'll not be knowing;
Yet there isn't a train I wouldn't take,
  No matter where it's going.

Low-Tide

These wet rocks where the tide has been,
  Barnacled white and weeded brown
And slimed beneath to a beautiful green,
  These wet rocks where the tide went down
Will show again when the tide is high
  Faint and perilous, far from shore,

No place to dream, but a place to die:
  The bottom of the sea once more.

There was a child that wandered through
  A giant's empty house all day,—
House full of wonderful things and new,
  But no fit place for a child to play!

Song of a Second April

April this year, not otherwise
  Than April of a year ago,
Is full of whispers, full of sighs,
  Of dazzling mud and dingy snow;
  Hepaticas that pleased you so
Are here again, and butterflies.

There rings a hammering all day,
  And shingles lie about the doors;
In orchards near and far away
  The grey wood-pecker taps and bores;
  And men are merry at their chores,
And children earnest at their play.

The larger streams run still and deep,
  Noisy and swift the small brooks run;

Among the mullein stalks the sheep
　　Go up the hillside in the sun,
　　Pensively,—only you are gone,
You that alone I cared to keep.

Rosemary

For the sake of some things
　　That be now no more
I will strew rushes
　　On my chamber-floor,
I will plant bergamot
　　At my kitchen-door.

For the sake of dim things
　　That were once so plain
I will set a barrel
　　Out to catch the rain,
I will hang an iron pot
　　On an iron crane.

Many things be dead and gone
　　That were brave and gay;
For the sake of these things
　　I will learn to say,
"An it please you, gentle sirs,"
　　"Alack!" and "Well-a-day!"

The Poet and His Book

Down, you mongrel, Death!
  Back into your kennel!
I have stolen breath
  In a stalk of fennel!
You shall scratch and you shall whine
  Many a night, and you shall worry
  Many a bone, before you bury
One sweet bone of mine!

When shall I be dead?
  When my flesh is withered,
And above my head
  Yellow pollen gathered
All the empty afternoon?
  When sweet lovers pause and wonder
  Who am I that lie thereunder,
Hidden from the moon?

This my personal death?—
  That my lungs be failing
To inhale the breath
  Others are exhaling?
This my subtle spirit's end?—
  Ah, when the thawed winter splashes
  Over these chance dust and ashes,
Weep not me, my friend!

Me, by no means dead
    In that hour, but surely
When this book, unread,
    Rots to earth obscurely,
And no more to any breast,
    Close against the clamorous swelling
    Of the thing there is no telling,
Are these pages pressed!

When this book is mould,
    And a book of many
Waiting to be sold
    For a casual penny,
In a little open case,
    In a street unclean and cluttered,
    Where a heavy mud is spattered
From the passing drays,

Stranger, pause and look;
    From the dust of ages
Lift this little book,
    Turn the tattered pages,
Read me, do not let me die!
    Search the fading letters, finding
    Steadfast in the broken binding
All that once was I!

When these veins are weeds,
　　When these hollowed sockets
Watch the rooty seeds
　　Bursting down like rockets,
And surmise the spring again,
　　Or, remote in that black cupboard,
　　Watch the pink worms writhing upward
At the smell of rain,

Boys and girls that lie
　　Whispering in the hedges,
Do not let me die,
　　Mix me with your pledges;
Boys and girls that slowly walk
　　In the woods, and weep, and quarrel,
　　Staring past the pink wild laurel,
Mix me with your talk,

Do not let me die!
　　Farmers at your raking,
When the sun is high,
　　While the hay is making,
When, along the stubble strewn,
　　Withering on their stalks uneaten,
　　Strawberries turn dark and sweeten
In the lapse of noon;

Shepherds on the hills,
   In the pastures, drowsing
To the tinkling bells
   Of the brown sheep browsing;
Sailors crying through the storm;
   Scholars at your study; hunters
   Lost amid the whirling winter's
Whiteness uniform;

Men that long for sleep;
   Men that wake and revel;—
If an old song leap
   To your senses' level
At such moments, may it be
   Sometimes, though a moment only,
   Some forgotten, quaint and homely
Vehicle of me!

Women at your toil,
   Women at your leisure
Till the kettle boil,
   Snatch of me your pleasure,
Where the broom-straw marks the leaf;
   Women quiet with your weeping
   Lest you wake a workman sleeping,
Mix me with your grief!

Boys and girls that steal
   From the shocking laughter
Of the old, to kneel
   By a dripping rafter
Under the discoloured eaves,
   Out of trunks with hingeless covers
   Lifting tales of saints and lovers,
Travellers, goblins, thieves,

Suns that shine by night,
   Mountains made from valleys,—
Bear me to the light,
   Flat upon your bellies
By the webby window lie,
   Where the little flies are crawling,
   Read me, margin me with scrawling,
Do not let me die!

Sexton, ply your trade!
   In a shower of gravel
Stamp upon your spade!
   Many a rose shall ravel,
Many a metal wreath shall rust
   In the rain, and I go singing
   Through the lots where you are flinging
Yellow clay on dust!

Alms

My heart is what it was before,
  A house where people come and go;
But it is winter with your love,
  The sashes are beset with snow.

I light the lamp and lay the cloth,
  I blow the coals to blaze again;
But it is winter with your love,
  The frost is thick upon the pane.

I know a winter when it comes:
  The leaves are listless on the boughs;
I watched your love a little while,
  And brought my plants into the house.

I water them and turn them south,
  I snap the dead brown from the stem;
But it is winter with your love,
  I only tend and water them.

There was a time I stood and watched
  The small, ill-natured sparrows' fray;
I loved the beggar that I fed,
  I cared for what he had to say.

I stood and watched him out of sight;
  Today I reach around the door
And set a bowl upon the step;
  My heart is what it was before,

But it is winter with your love;
 I scatter crumbs upon the sill,
And close the window,—and the birds
 May take or leave them, as they will.

Inland

People that build their houses inland,
 People that buy a plot of ground
Shaped like a house, and build a house there,
 Far from the sea-board, far from the sound

Of water sucking the hollow ledges,
 Tons of water striking the shore,—
What do they long for, as I long for
 One salt smell of the sea once more?

People the waves have not awakened,
 Spanking the boats at the harbour's head,
What do they long for, as I long for,—
 Starting up in my inland bed,

Beating the narrow walls, and finding
 Neither a window nor a door,
Screaming to God for death by drowning,—
 One salt taste of the sea once more?

To a Poet that Died Young

Minstrel, what have you to do
With this man that, after you,
Sharing not your happy fate,
Sat as England's Laureate?
Vainly, in these iron days,
Strives the poet in your praise,
Minstrel, by whose singing side
Beauty walked, until you died.

Still, though none should hark again,
Drones the blue-fly in the pane,
Thickly crusts the blackest moss,
Blows the rose its musk across,
Floats the boat that is forgot
None the less to Camelot.

Many a bard's untimely death
Lends unto his verses breath;
Here's a song was never sung:
Growing old is dying young.
Minstrel, what is this to you:
That a man you never knew,
When your grave was far and green,
Sat and gossipped with a queen?

Thalia knows how rare a thing
Is it, to grow old and sing,
When the brown and tepid tide
Closes in on every side.
Who shall say if Shelley's gold
Had withstood it to grow old?

Wraith

"Thin Rain, whom are you haunting,
    That you haunt my door?"
Surely it is not I she's wanting . . .
    Someone living here before!
"Nobody's in the house but me:
You may come in if you like and see."

Thin as thread, with exquisite fingers,—
    Ever seen her, any of you?—
Grey shawl, and leaning on the wind,
    And the garden showing through?

Glimmering eyes,—and silent, mostly,
    Sort of a whisper, sort of a purr,
Asking something, asking it over,
    If you get a sound from her.—

Ever see her, any of you?—
   Strangest thing I've ever known,—
Every night since I moved in,
   And I came to be alone.

"Thin Rain, hush with your knocking!
   You may not come in!
This is I that you hear rocking;
   Nobody's with me, nor has been!"

Curious, how she tried the window,—
   Odd, the way she tries the door,—
Wonder just what sort of people
   Could have had this house before . . .

Ebb

I know what my heart is like
   Since your love died:
It is like a hollow ledge
Holding a little pool
   Left there by the tide,
   A little tepid pool,
Drying inward from the edge.

Elaine

Oh, come again to Astolat!
    I will not ask you to be kind.
And you may go when you will go,
    And I will stay behind.

I will not say how dear you are,
    Or ask you if you hold me dear,
Or trouble you with things for you,
    The way I did last year.

So still the orchard, Lancelot,
    So very still the lake shall be,
You could not guess—though you should guess—
    What is become of me.

So wide shall be the garden-walk,
    The garden-seat so very wide,
You needs must think—if you should think—
    The lily maid had died.

Save that, a little way away,
    I'd watch you for a little while,
To see you speak, the way you speak,
    And smile,—if you should smile.

Burial

Mine is a body that should die at sea!
   And have for a grave, instead of a grave
Six feet deep and the length of me,
   All the water that is under the wave!

And terrible fishes to seize my flesh,
   Such as a living man might fear,
And eat me while I am firm and fresh,—
   Not wait till I've been dead for a year!

Mariposa

Butterflies are white and blue
In this field we wander through.
Suffer me to take your hand.
Death comes in a day or two.

All the things we ever knew
Will be ashes in that hour:
Mark the transient butterfly,
How he hangs upon the flower.

Suffer me to take your hand.
Suffer me to cherish you
Till the dawn is in the sky.
Whether I be false or true,
Death comes in a day or two.

The Little Hill

Oh, here the air is sweet and still,
   And soft's the grass to lie on;
And far away's the little hill
   They took for Christ to die on.

And there's a hill across the brook,
   And down the brook's another;
But, oh, the little hill they took,—
   I think I am its mother!

The moon that saw Gethsemane,
   I watch it rise and set;
It has so many things to see,
   They help it to forget.

But little hills that sit at home
   So many hundred years,
Remember Greece, remember Rome,
   Remember Mary's tears.

And far away in Palestine,
   Sadder than any other,
Grieves still the hill that I call mine,—
   I think I am its mother.

Doubt No More that Oberon

Doubt no more that Oberon—
Never doubt that Pan
Lived, and played a reed, and ran
After nymphs in a dark forest,
In the merry, credulous days,—
Lived, and led a fairy band
Over the indulgent land!

Ah, for in this dourest, sorest
Age man's eye has looked upon,
Death to fauns and death to fays,
Still the dog-wood dares to raise—
Healthy tree, with trunk and root—
Ivory bowls that bear no fruit,
And the starlings and the jays—
Birds that cannot even sing—
Dare to come again in spring!

Lament

Listen, children:
Your father is dead.
From his old coats
I'll make you little jackets;
I'll make you little trousers
From his old pants.

There'll be in his pockets
Things he used to put there,
Keys and pennies
Covered with tobacco;
Dan shall have the pennies
To save in his bank;
Anne shall have the keys
To make a pretty noise with.
Life must go on,
And the dead be forgotten;
Life must go on,
Though good men die;
Anne, eat your breakfast;
Dan, take your medicine;
Life must go on;
I forget just why.

Exiled

Searching my heart for its true sorrow,
    This is the thing I find to be:
That I am weary of words and people,
    Sick of the city, wanting the sea;

Wanting the sticky, salty sweetness
    Of the strong wind and shattered spray;
Wanting the loud sound and the soft sound
    Of the big surf that breaks all day.

Always before about my dooryard,
  Marking the reach of the winter sea,
Rooted in sand and dragging drift-wood,
  Straggled the purple wild sweet-pea;

Always I climbed the wave at morning,
  Shook the sand from my shoes at night,
That now am caught beneath great buildings,
  Stricken with noise, confused with light.

If I could hear the green piles groaning
  Under the windy wooden piers,
See once again the bobbing barrels,
  And the black sticks that fence the weirs,

If I could see the weedy mussels
  Crusting the wrecked and rotting hulls,
Hear once again the hungry crying
  Overhead, of the wheeling gulls,

Feel once again the shanty straining
  Under the turning of the tide,
Fear once again the rising freshet,
  Dread the bell in the fog outside,

I should be happy!—that was happy
  All day long on the coast of Maine;
I have a need to hold and handle
  Shells and anchors and ships again!

I should be happy . . . that am happy
  Never at all since I came here.
I am too long away from water.
  I have a need of water near.

The Death of Autumn

When reeds are dead and a straw to thatch the
    marshes,
And feathered pampas-grass rides into the wind
Like agèd warriors westward, tragic, thinned
Of half their tribe; and over the flattened rushes,
Stripped of its secret, open, stark and bleak,
Blackens afar the half-forgotten creek,—
Then leans on me the weight of the year, and crushes
My heart. I know that Beauty must ail and die,
And will be born again,—but ah, to see
Beauty stiffened, staring up at the sky!
Oh, Autumn! Autumn!—What is the Spring to me?

Ode to Silence

Aye, but she?
Your other sister and my other soul,
Grave Silence, lovelier
Than the three loveliest maidens, what of her?
Clio, not you,
Not you, Calliope,
Nor all your wanton line,
Not Great Apollo's self shall comfort me
For Silence once departed,
For her the cool-tongued, her the tranquil-hearted,
Whom evermore I follow wistfully,
Wandering Heaven and Earth and Hell and the four
    seasons through;
Thalia, not you,
Not you, Melpomene,
Not your incomparable feet, O thin Terpsichore,
I seek in this great hall,
But one more pale, more pensive, most beloved of
    you all.

I seek her from afar.
I come from temples where her altars are;
From groves that bear her name;—
Noisy with stricken victims now and sacrificial flame,

And cymbals struck on high and strident faces
Obstreperous in her praise
They neither love nor know,
A goddess of gone days,
Departed long ago,
Abandoning the invaded shrines and fanes
Of her old sanctuary,
A deity obscure and legendary,
Of whom there now remains,
For sages to decipher and priests to garble,
Only and for a little while her letters wedged in
　　　marble;
Which even now, behold, the friendly mumbling rain
　　　erases,
And the inarticulate snow,
Leaving at last of her least signs and traces
None whatsoever, nor whither she is vanished from
　　　these places.

"She will love well," I said,
"If love be of that heart inhabiter,
The flowers of the dead:
The red anemone that with no sound
Moves in the wind; and from another wound
That sprang, the heavily-sweet blue hyacinth,
That blossoms underground;
And sallow poppies, will be dear to her.
And will not Silence know
In the black shade of what obsidian steep
Stiffens the white narcissus numb with sleep?

(Seed which Demeter's daughter bore from home,
Uptorn by desperate fingers long ago,
Reluctant even as she,
Undone Persephone,
And even as she, set out again to grow,
In twilight, in perdition's lean and inauspicious loam)
She will love well," I said,
"The flowers of the dead.
Where dark Persephone the winter round,
Uncomforted for home, uncomforted,
Lacking a sunny southern slope in northern Sicily,
With sullen pupils focussed on a dream
Stares on the stagnant stream
That moats the unequivocable battlements of Hell,
There, there will she be found,
She that is Beauty veiled from men and Music in a
    swound."

"I long for Silence as they long for breath
Whose helpless nostrils drink the bitter sea;
What thing can be
So stout, what so redoubtable, in Death
What fury, what considerable rage, if only she,
Upon whose icy breast,
Unquestioned, uncaressed,
One time I lay,

And whom always I lack,
Even to this day,
Being by no means from that frigid bosom weaned
away,
If only she therewith be given me back?"

I sought her down that dolourous labyrinth,
Wherein no shaft of sunlight ever fell,
And in among the bloodless everywhere
I sought her; but the air,
Breathed many times and spent,
Was fretful with a whispering discontent;
And questioning me, importuning me to tell
Some slightest tidings of the light of day they know
no more,
Plucking my sleeve, the eager shades were with me
where I went.
I paused at every grievous door,
And harked a moment, holding up my hand,—and for
a space
A hush was on them, while they watched my face;
And then they fell a-whispering as before;
So that I smiled at them and left them, seeing she was
not there.

I sought her, too,
Among the upper gods, although I knew
She was not like to be where feasting is,
Nor near to Heaven's lord,

Being a thing abhorred
And shunned of him, although a child of his,
(Not yours, not yours: to you she owes not breath,
Mother of Song, being sown of Zeus upon a dream of
    Death).

Fearing to pass unvisited some place
And later learn, too late, how all the while,
With her still face,
She had been standing there and seen me pass, with-
    out a smile,
I sought her even to the sagging board whereat
The stout immortals sat;
But such a laughter shook the mighty hall
No one could hear me say:
Had she been seen upon the Hill that day?
And no one knew at all
How long I stood, or when at last I sighed and went
    away.

There is a garden lying in a lull
Between the mountains and the mountainous sea . . .
I know not where; but which a dream diurnal
Paints on my lids a moment, till the hull
Be lifted from the kernel,
And Slumber fed to me.
Your foot-print is not there, Mnemosene,

Though it would seem a ruined place and after
Your lichenous heart, being full
Of broken columns, caryatides
Thrown to the earth and fallen forward on their joint-
  less knees;
And urns funereal altered into dust
Minuter than the ashes of the dead;
And Psyche's lamp out of the earth up-thrust,
Dripping itself in marble oil on what was once the
  bed
Of Love, and his young body asleep, but now is dust
  instead.

There twists the bitter-sweet, the white wisteria
Fastens its fingers in the strangling wall,
And the wide crannies quicken with bright weeds;
There dumbly like a worm all day the still white
  orchid feeds;
But never an echo of your daughters' laughter
Is there, nor any sign of you at all
Swells fungous from the rotten bough, grey mother of
  Pieria!

Only her shadow once upon a stone
I saw,—and, lo, the shadow and the garden, too, were
  gone.

I tell you, you have done her body an ill,
You chatterers, you noisy crew!
She is not anywhere!

I sought her in deep Hell;
And through the world as well;
I thought of Heaven and I sought her there:
Above nor under ground
Is Silence to be found,
That was the very warp and woof of you,
Lovely before your songs began and after they were
    through!
Oh, say if on this hill
Somewhere your sister's body lies in death,
So I may follow there, and make a wreath
Of my locked hands, that on her quiet breast
Shall lie till age has withered them!

                    (Ah, sweetly from the rest
I see
Turn and consider me
Compassionate Euterpe!)

"There is a gate beyond the gate of Death,
Beyond the gate of everlasting Life,
Beyond the gates of Heaven and Hell," she saith,
"Whereon but to believe is horror!
Whereon to meditate engendereth
Even in deathless spirits such as I
A tumult in the breath,
A chilling of the inexhaustible blood
Even in my veins that never will be dry,

And in the austere, divine monotony
That is my being, the madness of an unaccustomed
   mood.

This is her province whom you lack and seek:
And seek her not elsewhere.
Hell is a thoroughfare
For pilgrims,—Herakles,
And he that loved Euridice too well,
Have walked therein; and many more than these;
And witnessed the desire and the despair
Of souls that passed reluctantly and sicken for the
   air;
You, too, have entered Hell,
And issued thence; but thence whereof I speak
None has returned;—for thither fury brings
Only the driven ghosts of them that flee before all
   things.
Oblivion is the name of this abode: and she is
   there."

O radiant Song! O gracious Memory!
Be long upon this height
I shall not climb again!
I know the way you mean,—the little night,
And the long empty day,—never to see
Again the angry light,
Or hear the hungry noises cry my brain!

Ah, but she,
Your other sister and my other soul,
She shall again be mine.
And I shall drink her from a silver bowl,
A chilly thin green wine,
Not bitter to the taste,
Not sweet,
Not of your press, O restless, clamourous Nine,—
To foam beneath the frantic hoofs of mirth—
But savouring faintly of the acid earth
And trod by pensive feet
From perfect clusters ripened without haste
Out of the urgent heat
In some clear glimmering vaulted twilight under the
odourous vine.

Lift up your lyres! Sing on!
But as for me, I seek your sister whither she is gone.

MEMORIAL TO D. C.

(Vassar College, 1918)

O, loveliest throat of all sweet throats,
Where now no more the music is,
With hands that wrote you little notes
I write you little elegies!

I

Epitaph

Heap not on this mound
   Roses that she loved so well;
Why bewilder her with roses,
   That she cannot see or smell?

She is happy where she lies
   With the dust upon her eyes.

II

Prayer to Persephone

Be to her, Persephone,
All the things I might not be;
Take her head upon your knee.
She that was so proud and wild,
Flippant, arrogant and free,
She that had no need of me,
Is a little lonely child
Lost in Hell,—Persephone,
Take her head upon your knee;
Say to her, "My dear, my dear,
It is not so dreadful here."

III

Chorus

Give away her gowns,
Give away her shoes;
She has no more use
For her fragrant gowns;
Take them all down,
Blue, green, blue,
Lilac, pink, blue,
From their padded hangers;

She will dance no more
In her narrow shoes;
Sweep her narrow shoes
From the closet floor.

IV

Dirge

Boys and girls that held her dear,
   Do your weeping now;
All you loved of her lies here.

Brought to earth the arrogant brow,
   And the withering tongue
Chastened; do your weeping now.

Sing whatever songs are sung,
   Wind whatever wreath,
For a playmate perished young,
   For a spirit spent in death.

Boys and girls that held her dear,
All you loved of her lies here.

Elegy

Let them bury your big eyes
In the secret earth securely,
Your thin fingers, and your fair,
Soft, indefinite-coloured hair,—
All of these in some way, surely,
From the secret earth shall rise;
Not for these I sit and stare,
Broken and bereft completely:
Your young flesh that sat so neatly
On your little bones will sweetly
Blossom in the air.

But your voice . . . never the rushing
Of a river underground,
Not the rising of the wind
In the trees before the rain,
Not the woodcock's watery call,
Not the note the white-throat utters,
Not the feet of children pushing
Yellow leaves along the gutters
In the blue and bitter fall,
Shall content my musing mind
For the beauty of that sound
That in no new way at all
Ever will be heard again.

Sweetly through the sappy stalk
Of the vigourous weed,
Holding all it held before,
Cherished by the faithful sun,
On and on eternally
Shall your altered fluid run,
Bud and bloom and go to seed:
But your singing days are done;
But the music of your talk
Never shall the chemistry
Of the secret earth restore.
All your lovely words are spoken.
Once the ivory box is broken,
Beats the golden bird no more.

Wild Swans

I looked in my heart while the wild swans went over.
And what did I see I had not seen before?
Only a question less or a question more;
Nothing to match the flight of wild birds flying.
Tiresome heart, forever living and dying,
House without air, I leave you and lock your door.
Wild swans, come over the town, come over
The town again, trailing your legs and crying!

From *A FEW FIGS*
FROM THISTLES

First Fig

My candle burns at both ends;
    It will not last the night;
But ah, my foes, and oh, my friends—
    It gives a lovely light!

Second Fig

Safe upon the solid rock the ugly houses stand:
Come and see my shining palace built upon the sand!

Recuerdo

We were very tired, we were very merry—
We had gone back and forth all night on the ferry.
It was bare and bright, and smelled like a stable—
But we looked into a fire, we leaned across a table,
We lay on a hill-top underneath the moon;
And the whistles kept blowing, and the dawn came
    soon.

We were very tired, we were very merry—
We had gone back and forth all night on the ferry;
And you ate an apple, and I ate a pear,
From a dozen of each we had bought somewhere;

And the sky went wan, and the wind came cold,
And the sun rose dripping, a bucketful of gold.

We were very tired, we were very merry,
We had gone back and forth all night on the ferry.
We hailed, "Good morrow, mother!" to a shawl-
covered head,
And bought a morning paper, which neither of us
read;
And she wept, "God bless you!" for the apples and
pears,
And we gave her all our money but our subway fares.

Thursday

And if I loved you Wednesday,
  Well, what is that to you?
I do not love you Thursday—
  So much is true.

And why you come complaining
  Is more than I can see.
I loved you Wednesday,—yes—but what
  Is that to me?

To the Not Impossible Him

How shall I know, unless I go
    To Cairo and Cathay,
Whether or not this blessèd spot
    Is blest in every way?

Now it may be, the flower for me
    Is this beneath my nose;
How shall I tell, unless I smell
    The Carthaginian rose?

The fabric of my faithful love
    No power shall dim or ravel
Whilst I stay here,—but oh, my dear,
    If I should ever travel!

Macdougal Street

As I went walking up and down to take the evening
    air,
    (Sweet to meet upon the street, why must I be so
      shy?)
I saw him lay his hand upon her torn black hair;
    ("Little dirty Latin child, let the lady by!")

The women squatting on the stoops were slovenly and
    fat,
  (Lay me out in organdie, lay me out in lawn!)
And everywhere I stepped there was a baby or a cat;
  (Lord God in Heaven, will it never be dawn?)

The fruit-carts and clam-carts were ribald as a fair,
  (Pink nets and wet shells trodden under heel)
She had haggled from the fruit-man of his rotting
    ware;
  (I shall never get to sleep, the way I feel!)

He walked like a king through the filth and the
    clutter,
  (Sweet to meet upon the street, why did you glance
    me by?)
But he caught the quaint Italian quip she flung him
    from the gutter;
  (What can there be to cry about that I should lie
    and cry?)

He laid his darling hand upon her little black head,
  (I wish I were a ragged child with ear-rings in my
    ears!)
And he said she was a baggage to have said what she
    had said;
  (Truly I shall be ill unless I stop these tears!)

The Singing-Woman from the Wood's Edge

What should I be but a prophet and a liar,
Whose mother was a leprechaun, whose father was a
    friar?
Teethed on a crucifix and cradled under water,
What should I be but the fiend's god-daughter?

And who should be my playmates but the adder and
    the frog,
That was got beneath a furze-bush and born in a bog?
And what should be my singing, that was christened at
    an altar,
But Aves and Credos and Psalms out of the Psalter?

You will see such webs on the wet grass, maybe,
As a pixie-mother weaves for her baby,
You will find such flame at the wave's weedy ebb
As flashes in the meshes of a mer-mother's web.

But there comes to birth no common spawn
From the love of a priest for a leprechaun,
And you never have seen and you never will see
Such things as the things that swaddled me!

After all's said and after all's done,
What should I be but a harlot and a nun?

In through the bushes, on any foggy day,
My Da would come a-swishing of the drops away,
With a prayer for my death and a groan for my birth,
A-mumbling of his beads for all that he was worth.

And there'd sit my Ma, with her knees beneath her
    chin,
A-looking in his face and a-drinking of it in,
And a-marking in the moss some funny little saying
That would mean just the opposite of all that he was
    praying!

He taught me the holy-talk of Vesper and of Matin,
He heard me my Greek and he heard me my Latin,
He blessed me and crossed me to keep my soul from
    evil,
And we watched him out of sight, and we conjured up
    the devil!

Oh, the things I haven't seen and the things I haven't
    known,
What with hedges and ditches till after I was grown,
And yanked both ways by my mother and my father,
With a "Which would you better?" and a "Which
    would you rather?"

With him for a sire and her for a dam,
What should I be but just what I am?

She Is Overheard Singing

Oh, Prue she has a patient man,
   And Joan a gentle lover,
And Agatha's Arth' is a hug-the-hearth,—
   But my true love's a rover!

Mig, her man's as good as cheese
   And honest as a briar,
Sue tells her love what he's thinking of,—
   But my dear lad's a liar!

Oh, Sue and Prue and Agatha
   Are thick with Mig and Joan!
They bite their threads and shake their heads
   And gnaw my name like a bone;

And Prue says, "Mine's a patient man,
   As never snaps me up,"
And Agatha, "Arth' is a hug-the-hearth,
   Could live content in a cup;"

Sue's man's mind is like good jell—
   All one color, and clear—
And Mig's no call to think at all
   What's to come next year,

While Joan makes boast of a gentle lad,
   That's troubled with that and this;—
But they all would give the life they live
   For a look from the man I kiss!

Cold he slants his eyes about,
    And few enough's his choice,—
Though he'd slip me clean for a nun, or a queen,
    Or a beggar with knots in her voice,—

And Agatha will turn awake
    While her good man sleeps sound,
And Mig and Sue and Joan and Prue
    Will hear the clock strike round,

For Prue she has a patient man,
    As asks not when or why,
And Mig and Sue have naught to do
    But peep who's passing by,

Joan is paired with a putterer
    That bastes and tastes and salts,
And Agatha's Arth' is a hug-the-hearth,—
    But my true love is false!

The Unexplorer

There was a road ran past our house
Too lovely to explore.
I asked my mother once—she said
That if you followed where it led
It brought you to the milk-man's door.
(That's why I have not travelled more.)

102

Grown-up

Was it for this I uttered prayers,
And sobbed and cursed and kicked the stairs,
That now, domestic as a plate,
I should retire at half-past eight?

The Penitent

I had a little Sorrow,
    Born of a little Sin,
I found a room all damp with gloom
    And shut us all within;
And, "Little Sorrow, weep," said I,
"And, Little Sin, pray God to die,
And I upon the floor will lie
    And think how bad I've been!"

Alas for pious planning—
    It mattered not a whit!
As far as gloom went in that room,
    The lamp might have been lit!
My little Sorrow would not weep,
My little Sin would go to sleep—
To save my soul I could not keep
    My graceless mind on it!

So up I got in anger,
    And took a book I had,
And put a ribbon on my hair
    To please a passing lad,
And, "One thing there's no getting by—
I've been a wicked girl," said I;
"But if I can't be sorry, why,
    I might as well be glad!"

Daphne

Why do you follow me?—
Any moment I can be
Nothing but a laurel-tree.

Any moment of the chase
I can leave you in my place
A pink bough for your embrace.

Yet if over hill and hollow
Still it is your will to follow,
I am off;—to heel, Apollo!

Portrait by a Neighbour

Before she has her floor swept
    Or her dishes done,
Any day you'll find her
    A-sunning in the sun!

It's long after midnight
    Her key's in the lock,
And you never see her chimney smoke
    Till past ten o'clock!

She digs in her garden
    With a shovel and a spoon,
She weeds her lazy lettuce
    By the light of the moon,

She walks up the walk
    Like a woman in a dream,
She forgets she borrowed butter
    And pays you back cream!

Her lawn looks like a meadow,
    And if she mows the place
She leaves the clover standing
    And the Queen Anne's lace!

Midnight Oil

Cut if you will, with Sleep's dull knife,
    Each day to half its length, my friend,—
The years that Time takes off *my* life,
    He'll take from off the other end!

The Merry Maid

Oh, I am grown so free from care
    Since my heart broke!
I set my throat against the air,
    I laugh at simple folk!

There's little kind and little fair
    Is worth its weight in smoke
To me, that's grown so free from care
    Since my heart broke!

Lass, if to sleep you would repair
    As peaceful as you woke,
Best not besiege your lover there
    For just the words he spoke
To me, that's grown so free from care
    Since my heart broke!

To Kathleen

Still must the poet as of old,
In barren attic bleak and cold,
Starve, freeze, and fashion verses to
Such things as flowers and song and you;

Still as of old his being give
In Beauty's name, while she may live,
Beauty that may not die as long
As there are flowers and you and song.

To S. M.

(If He Should Lie A-dying)

I am not willing you should go
Into the earth, where Helen went;
She is awake by now, I know.
Where Cleopatra's anklets rust
You will not lie with my consent;
And Sappho is a roving dust;
Cressid could love again; Dido,
Rotted in state, is restless still:
You leave me much against my will.

The Philosopher

And what are you that, wanting you,
    I should be kept awake
As many nights as there are days
    With weeping for your sake?

And what are you that, missing you,
    As many days as crawl
I should be listening to the wind
    And looking at the wall?

I know a man that's a braver man
    And twenty men as kind,
And what are you, that you should be
    The one man in my mind?

Yet women's ways are witless ways,
    As any sage will tell,—
And what am I, that I should love
    So wisely and so well?

From *THE HARP-WEAVER
AND OTHER POEMS*

My Heart, Being Hungry

My heart, being hungry, feeds on food
   The fat of heart despise.
Beauty where beauty never stood,
   And sweet where no sweet lies
I gather to my querulous need,
Having a growing heart to feed.

It may be, when my heart is dull,
   Having attained its girth,
I shall not find so beautiful
   The meagre shapes of earth,
Nor linger in the rain to mark
The smell of tansy through the dark.

Autumn Chant

Now the autumn shudders
   In the rose's root.
Far and wide the ladders
   Lean among the fruit.

Now the autumn clambers
   Up the trellised frame,
And the rose remembers
   The dust from which it came.

Brighter than the blossom
  On the rose's bough
Sits the wizened orange,
  Bitter berry now;

Beauty never slumbers;
  All is in her name;
But the rose remembers
  The dust from which it came.

Nuit Blanche

I am a shepherd of those sheep
  That climb a wall by night,
One after one, until I sleep,
  Or the black pane goes white.
Because of which I cannot see
  A flock upon a hill,
But doubts come tittering up to me
  That should by day be still.
And childish griefs I have outgrown
  Into my eyes are thrust,
Till my dull tears go dropping down
  Like lead into the dust.

Three Songs from "The Lamp and the Bell"

I

Oh, little rose tree, bloom!
Summer is nearly over.
The dahlias bleed, and the phlox is seed.
Nothing's left of the clover.
And the path of the poppy no one knows.
I would blossom if I were a rose.

Summer, for all your guile,
Will brown in a week to Autumn,
And launched leaves throw a shadow below
Over the brook's clear bottom,—
And the chariest bud the year can boast
Be brought to bloom by the chastening frost.

II

Beat me a crown of bluer metal;
   Fret it with stones of a foreign style:
The heart grows weary after a little
   Of what it loved for a little while.

Weave me a robe of richer fibre;
   Pattern its web with a rare device:
Give away to the child of a neighbour
   This gold gown I was glad in twice.

But buy me a singer to sing one song—
    Song about nothing—song about sheep—
Over and over, all day long;
    Patch me again my thread-bare sleep.

III

Rain comes down
And hushes the town.
And where is the voice that I heard crying?

Snow settles
Over the nettles.
Where is the voice that I heard crying?

Sand at last
On the drifting mast.
And where is the voice that I heard crying?

Earth now
On the busy brow.
And where is the voice that I heard crying?

The Wood Road

If I were to walk this way
    Hand in hand with Grief,
I should mark that maple-spray
    Coming into leaf.

I should note how the old burrs
  Rot upon the ground.
Yes, though Grief should know me hers
  While the world goes round,
It could not in truth be said
  This was lost on me:
A rock-maple showing red,
  Burrs beneath a tree.

Feast

I drank at every vine.
  The last was like the first.
I came upon no wine
  So wonderful as thirst.

I gnawed at every root.
  I ate of every plant.
I came upon no fruit
  So wonderful as want.

Feed the grape and bean
  To the vintner and monger;
I will lie down lean
  With my thirst and my hunger.

Souvenir

Just a rainy day or two
In a windy tower,
That was all I had of you—
Saving half an hour

Marred by greeting passing groups
In a cinder walk,
Near some naked blackberry hoops
Dim with purple chalk.

I remember three or four
Things you said in spite,
And an ugly coat you wore,
Plaided black and white.

Just a rainy day or two
And a bitter word.
Why do I remember you
As a singing bird?

Scrub

If I grow bitterly,
Like a gnarled and stunted tree,
Bearing harshly of my youth
Puckered fruit that sears the mouth;

If I make of my drawn boughs
An inhospitable house,
Out of which I never pry
Towards the water and the sky,
Under which I stand and hide
And hear the day go by outside;
It is that a wind too strong
Bent my back when I was young,
It is that I fear the rain
Lest it blister me again.

The Goose-Girl

Spring rides no horses down the hill,
But comes on foot, a goose-girl still.
And all the loveliest things there be
Come simply, so, it seems to me.
If ever I said, in grief or pride,
I tired of honest things, I lied;
And should be cursed forevermore
With Love in laces, like a whore,
And neighbours cold, and friends unsteady,
And Spring on horseback, like a lady!

The Dragonfly

I wound myself in a white cocoon of singing,
  All day long in the brook's uneven bed,
  Measuring out my soul in a mucous thread;
Dimly now to the brook's green bottom clinging,
  Men behold me, a worm spun-out and dead,
Walled in an iron house of silky singing.

Nevertheless at length, O reedy shallows,
  Not as a plodding nose to the slimy stem,
  But as a brazen wing with a spangled hem,
Over the jewel-weed and the pink marshmallows,
  Free of these and making a song of them,
I shall arise, and a song of the reedy shallows!

Departure

It's little I care what path I take,
And where it leads it's little I care;
But out of this house, lest my heart break,
I must go, and off somewhere.

It's little I know what's in my heart,
What's in my mind it's little I know,
But there's that in me must up and start,
And it's little I care where my feet go.

I wish I could walk for a day and a night,
And find me at dawn in a desolate place
With never the rut of a road in sight,
Nor the roof of a house, nor the eyes of a face.

I wish I could walk till my blood should spout,
And drop me, never to stir again,
On a shore that is wide, for the tide is out,
And the weedy rocks are bare to the rain.

But dump or dock, where the path I take
Brings up, it's little enough I care;
And it's little I'd mind the fuss they'll make,
Huddled dead in a ditch somewhere.

"Is something the matter, dear," she said,
"That you sit at your work so silently?"
"No, mother, no, 'twas a knot in my thread.
There goes the kettle, I'll make the tea."

The Return from Town

As I sat down by Saddle Stream
  To bathe my dusty feet there,
A boy was standing on the bridge
  Any girl would meet there.

As I went over Woody Knob
  And dipped into the hollow,
A youth was coming up the hill
  Any maid would follow.

Then in I turned at my own gate,—
  And nothing to be sad for—
To such a man as any wife
  Would pass a pretty lad for.

A Visit to the Asylum

Once from a big, big building,
When I was small, small,
The queer folk in the windows
Would smile at me and call.

And in the hard wee gardens
Such pleasant men would hoe:
"Sir, may we touch the little girl's hair!"—
It was so red, you know.

They cut me coloured asters
With shears so sharp and neat,
They brought me grapes and plums and pears
And pretty cakes to eat.

And out of all the windows,
No matter where we went,
The merriest eyes would follow me
And make me compliment.

There were a thousand windows,
All latticed up and down.
And up to all the windows,
When we went back to town,

The queer folk put their faces,
As gentle as could be;
"Come again, little girl!" they called, and I
Called back, "You come see me!"

The Spring and the Fall

In the spring of the year, in the spring of the year,
I walked the road beside my dear.
The trees were black where the bark was wet.
I see them yet, in the spring of the year.
He broke me a bough of the blossoming peach
That was out of the way and hard to reach.

In the fall of the year, in the fall of the year,
I walked the road beside my dear.
The rooks went up with a raucous trill.
I hear them still, in the fall of the year.
He laughed at all I dared to praise,
And broke my heart, in little ways.

Year be springing or year be falling,
The bark will drip and the birds be calling.
There's much that's fine to see and hear
In the spring of a year, in the fall of a year.
'Tis not love's going hurts my days,
But that it went in little ways.

The Curse

Oh, lay my ashes on the wind
That blows across the sea.
And I shall meet a fisherman
Out of Capri,

And he will say, seeing me,
"What a strange thing!
Like a fish's scale or a
Butterfly's wing."

Oh, lay my ashes on the wind
That blows away the fog.
And I shall meet a farmer boy
Leaping through the bog,

And he will say, seeing me,
"What a strange thing!
Like a peat-ash or a
Butterfly's wing."

And I shall blow to your house
And, sucked against the pane,
See you take your sewing up
And lay it down again.

And you will say, seeing me,
"What a strange thing!
Like a plum petal or a
Butterfly's wing."

And none at all will know me
That knew me well before.
But I will settle at the root
That climbs about your door,

And fishermen and farmers
May see me and forget,
But I'll be a bitter berry
In your brewing yet.

Keen

Weep him dead and mourn as you may,
　Me, I sing as I must:
Blessèd be Death, that cuts in marble
　What would have sunk to dust!

Blessèd be Death, that took my love
　And buried him in the sea,
Where never a lie nor a bitter word
　Will out of his mouth at me.

This I have to hold to my heart,
   This to take by the hand:
Sweet we were for a summer month
   As the sun on the dry white sand;

Mild we were for a summer month
   As the wind from over the weirs.
And blessèd be Death, that hushed with salt
   The harsh and slovenly years!

Who builds her a house with love for timber
   Builds her a house of foam.
And I'd liefer be bride to a lad gone down
   Than widow to one safe home.

The Betrothal

Oh, come, my lad, or go, my lad,
And love me if you like.
I shall not hear the door shut
Nor the knocker strike.

Oh, bring me gifts or beg me gifts,
And wed me if you will.
I'd make a man a good wife,
Sensible and still.

And why should I be cold, my lad,
And why should you repine,
Because I love a dark head
That never will be mine?

I might as well be easing you
As lie alone in bed
And waste the night in wanting
A cruel dark head.

You might as well be calling yours
What never will be his,
And one of us be happy.
There's few enough as is.

Humoresque

"Heaven bless the babe!" they said.
"What queer books she must have read!"
(Love, by whom I was beguiled,
Grant I may not bear a child.)

"Little does she guess to-day
What the world may be!" they say.
(Snow, drift deep and cover
Till the spring my murdered lover.)

The Pond

In this pond of placid water,
    Half a hundred years ago,
So they say, a farmer's daughter,
    Jilted by her farmer beau,

Waded out among the rushes,
    Scattering the blue dragon-flies;
That dried stick the ripple washes
    Marks the spot, I should surmise.

Think, so near the public highway,
    Well frequented even then!
Can you not conceive the sly way,—
    Hearing wheels or seeing men

Passing on the road above,—
    With a gesture feigned and silly,
Ere she drowned herself for love,
    She would reach to pluck a lily?

The Ballad of the Harp-Weaver

"Son," said my mother,
  When I was knee-high,
"You've need of clothes to cover you,
  And not a rag have I.

"There's nothing in the house
  To make a boy breeches,
Nor shears to cut a cloth with,
  Nor thread to take stitches.

"There's nothing in the house
  But a loaf-end of rye,
And a harp with a woman's head
  Nobody will buy,"
  And she began to cry.

That was in the early fall.
  When came the late fall,
"Son," she said, "the sight of you
  Makes your mother's blood crawl,—

"Little skinny shoulder-blades
  Sticking through your clothes!
And where you'll get a jacket from
  God above knows.

"It's lucky for me, lad,
  Your daddy's in the ground,
And can't see the way I let
  His son go around!"
    And she made a queer sound.

That was in the late fall.
  When the winter came,
I'd not a pair of breeches
  Nor a shirt to my name.

I couldn't go to school,
  Or out of doors to play.
And all the other little boys
  Passed our way.

"Son," said my mother,
  "Come, climb into my lap,
And I'll chafe your little bones
  While you take a nap."

And, oh, but we were silly
  For half an hour or more,
Me with my long legs
  Dragging on the floor.

A-rock-rock-rocking
  To a mother-goose rhyme!
Oh, but we were happy
  For half an hour's time!

But there was I, a great boy,
  And what would folks say
To hear my mother singing me
  To sleep all day,
  In such a daft way?

Men say the winter
  Was bad that year;
Fuel was scarce,
  And food was dear.

A wind with a wolf's head
  Howled about our door,
And we burned up the chairs
  And sat upon the floor.

All that was left us
  Was a chair we couldn't break,
And the harp with a woman's head
  Nobody would take,
  For song or pity's sake.

The night before Christmas
  I cried with the cold,
I cried myself to sleep
  Like a two-year-old.

And in the deep night
   I felt my mother rise,
And stare down upon me
   With love in her eyes.

I saw my mother sitting
   On the one good chair,
A light falling on her
   From I couldn't tell where,

Looking nineteen,
   And not a day older,
And the harp with a woman's head
   Leaned against her shoulder.

Her thin fingers, moving
   In the thin, tall strings,
Were weav-weav-weaving
   Wonderful things.

Many bright threads,
   From where I couldn't see,
Were running through the harp-strings
   Rapidly,

And gold threads whistling
   Through my mother's hand.
I saw the web grow,
   And the pattern expand.

She wove a child's jacket,
    And when it was done
She laid it on the floor
    And wove another one.

She wove a red cloak
    So regal to see,
"She's made it for a king's son,"
    I said, "and not for me."
    But I knew it was for me.

She wove a pair of breeches
    Quicker than that!
She wove a pair of boots
    And a little cocked hat.

She wove a pair of mittens,
    She wove a little blouse,
She wove all night
    In the still, cold house.

She sang as she worked,
    And the harp-strings spoke;
Her voice never faltered,
    And the thread never broke.
    And when I awoke,—

There sat my mother
    With the harp against her shoulder,
Looking nineteen,
    And not a day older,

A smile about her lips,
  And a light about her head,
And her hands in the harp-strings
  Frozen dead.

And piled up beside her
  And toppling to the skies,
Were the clothes of a king's son,
  Just my size.

Never May the Fruit Be Plucked

Never, never may the fruit be plucked from the
    bough
And gathered into barrels.
He that would eat of love must eat it where it hangs.
Though the branches bend like reeds,
Though the ripe fruit splash in the grass or wrinkle on
    the tree,
He that would eat of love may bear away with him
Only what his belly can hold,
Nothing in the apron,
Nothing in the pockets.
Never, never may the fruit be gathered from the
    bough
And harvested in barrels.
The winter of love is a cellar of empty bins,
In an orchard soft with rot.

The Concert

No, I will go alone.
I will come back when it's over.
Yes, of course I love you.
No, it will not be long.
Why may you not come with me?—
You are too much my lover.
You would put yourself
Between me and song.

If I go alone,
Quiet and suavely clothed,
My body will die in its chair,
And over my head a flame,
A mind that is twice my own,
Will mark with icy mirth
The wise advance and retreat
Of armies without a country,
Storming a nameless gate,
Hurling terrible javelins down
From the shouting walls of a singing town
Where no women wait!
Armies clean of love and hate,
Marching lines of pitiless sound
Climbing hills to the sun and hurling
Golden spears to the ground!
Up the lines a silver runner
Bearing a banner whereon is scored
The milk and steel of a bloodless wound
Healed at length by the sword!

You and I have nothing to do with music.
We may not make of music a filigree frame,
Within which you and I,
Tenderly glad we came,
Sit smiling, hand in hand.

Come now, be content.
I will come back to you, I swear I will;
And you will know me still.
I shall be only a little taller
Than when I went.

Hyacinth

I am in love with him to whom a hyacinth is dearer
Than I shall ever be dear.
On nights when the field-mice are abroad he cannot
sleep:
He hears their narrow teeth at the bulbs of his hya-
cinths.
But the gnawing at my heart he does not hear.

To One Who Might Have Borne a Message

Had I known that you were going
I would have given you messages for her,
Now two years dead,
Whom I shall always love.

As it is, should she entreat you how it goes with me,
You must reply: as well as with most, you fancy;
That I love easily, and pass the time.

And she will not know how all day long between
My life and me her shadow intervenes,
A young thin girl,
Wearing a white skirt and a purple sweater
And a narrow pale blue ribbon about her hair.

I used to say to her, "I love you
Because your face is such a pretty color,
No other reason."
But it was not true.

Oh, had I only known that you were going,
I could have given you messages for her!

Siege

This I do, being mad:
Gather baubles about me,

Sit in a circle of toys, and all the time
Death beating the door in.

White jade and an orange pitcher,
Hindu idol, Chinese god,—
Maybe next year, when I'm richer—
Carved beads and a lotus pod. . . .

And all this time
Death beating the door in.

The Cairn

When I think of the little children learning
In all the schools of the world,
Learning in Danish, learning in Japanese
That two and two are four, and where the rivers of the
    world
Rise, and the names of the mountains and the prin-
    cipal cities,
My heart breaks.
Come up, children! Toss your little stones gaily
On the great cairn of Knowledge!
(Where lies what Euclid knew, a little grey stone,
What Plato, what Pascal, what Galileo:
Little grey stones, little grey stones on a cairn.)
Tell me, what is the name of the highest mountain?
Name me a crater of fire! a peak of snow!
Name me the mountains on the moon!
But the name of the mountain that you climb all day,
Ask not your teacher that.

Spring Song

I know why the yellow forsythia
Holds its breath and will not bloom,
And the robin thrusts his beak in his wing.

Want me to tell you? Think you can bear it?
Cover your eyes with your hand and hear it.
You know how cold the days are still?
And everybody saying how late the Spring is?
Well—cover your eyes with your hand—the thing is,
There isn't going to be any Spring.

No parking here! No parking here!
They said to Spring: No parking here!

Spring came on as she always does,
Laid her hand on the yellow forsythia,—
Little boys turned in their sleep and smiled,
Dreaming of marbles, dreaming of agates;
Little girls leapt from their beds to see
Spring come by with her painted wagons,
Coloured wagons creaking with wonder—
Laid her hand on the robin's throat;
When up comes you-know-who, my dear,
You-know-who in a fine blue coat,
And says to Spring: No parking here!

No parking here! No parking here!
Move on! Move on! No parking here!

Come walk with me in the city gardens.
(Better keep an eye out for you-know-who)
Did ever you see such a sickly showing?—
Middle of June, and nothing growing;
The gardeners peer and scratch their heads
And drop their sweat on the tulip-beds,
But not a blade thrusts through.

Come, move on! Don't you know how to walk?
No parking here! And no back-talk!

Oh, well,—hell, it's all for the best.
She certainly made a lot of clutter,
Dropping petals under the trees,
Taking your mind off your bread and butter.
Anyhow, it's nothing to me.
I can remember, and so can you.
(Though we'd better watch out for you-know-who,
When we sit around remembering Spring).

We shall hardly notice in a year or two.
You can get accustomed to anything.

Memory of Cape Cod

The wind in the ash-tree sounds like surf on the shore
    at Truro.
I will shut my eyes . . . hush, be still with your silly
    bleating, sheep on Shillingstone Hill . . .

*They said: Come along! They said: Leave your pebbles
    on the sand and come along, it's long after sunset!*
*The mosquitoes will be thick in the pine-woods along
    by Long Nook, the wind's died down!*
*They said: Leave your pebbles on the sand, and your
    shells, too, and come along, we'll find you another
    beach like the beach at Truro.*

Let me listen to wind in the ash . . . it sounds like
    surf on the shore.

From *THE BUCK*
IN THE SNOW

Moriturus

If I could have
   Two things in one:
The peace of the grave,
   And the light of the sun;

My hands across
   My thin breast-bone,
But aware of the moss
   Invading the stone,

Aware of the flight
   Of the golden flicker
With his wing to the light;
   To hear him nicker

And drum with his bill
   On the rotted willow;
Snug and still
   On a grey pillow

Deep in the clay
   Where digging is hard,
Out of the way,—
   The blue shard

Of a broken platter—
  If I might be
Insensate matter
  With sensate me

Sitting within,
  Harking and prying,
I might begin
  To dicker with dying.

For the body at best
  Is a bundle of aches,
Longing for rest;
  It cries when it wakes

"Alas, 'tis light!"
  At set of sun
"Alas, 'tis night,
  And nothing done!"

Death, however,
  Is a spongy wall,
Is a sticky river,
  Is nothing at all.

Summon the weeper,
  Wail and sing;
Call him Reaper,
  Angel, King;

Call him Evil
  Drunk to the lees,
Monster, Devil,—
  He is less than these.

Call him Thief,
  The Maggot in the Cheese,
The Canker in the Leaf,—
  He is less than these.

Dusk without sound,
  Where the spirit by pain
Uncoiled, is wound
  To spring again;

The mind enmeshed
  Laid straight in repose,
And the body refreshed
  By feeding the rose,—

These are but visions;
   These would be
The grave's derisions,
   Could the grave see.

Here is the wish
   Of one that died
Like a beached fish
   On the ebb of the tide:

That he might wait
   Till the tide came back,
To see if a crate,
   Or a bottle, or a black

Boot, or an oar,
   Or an orange peel
Be washed ashore. . . .
   About his heel

The sand slips;
   The last he hears
From the world's lips
   Is the sand in his ears.

What thing is little?—
    The aphis hid
In a house of spittle?
    The hinge of the lid

Of the spider's eye
    At the spider's birth?
"Greater am I
    By the earth's girth

Than Mighty Death!"
    All creatures cry
That can summon breath;—
    And speak no lie.

For He is nothing;
    He is less
Than Echo answering
    "Nothingness!"—

Less than the heat
    Of the furthest star
To the ripening wheat;
    Less by far,

When all the lipping
  Is said and sung,
Than the sweat dripping
  From the dog's tongue.

This being so,
  And I being such,
I would liever go
  On a cripple's crutch,

Lopped and felled;
  Liever be dependent
On a chair propelled
  By a surly attendant

With a foul breath,
  And be spooned my food,
Than go with Death
  Where nothing good,

Not even the thrust
  Of the summer gnat,
Consoles the dust
  For being that.

Needy, lonely,
   Stitched by pain,
Left with only
   The drip of the rain

Out of all I had;
   The books of the wise,
Badly read
   By other eyes,

Lewdly bawled
   At my closing ear;
Hated, called
   A lingerer here;—

Withstanding Death
   Till Life be gone,
I shall treasure my breath,
   I shall linger on.

I shall bolt my door
   With a bolt and a cable;
I shall block my door
   With a bureau and a table;

With all my might
   My door shall be barred.
I shall put up a fight,
   I shall take it hard.

With his hand on my mouth
   He shall drag me forth,
Shrieking to the south
   And clutching at the north.

Song

Gone, gone again is Summer the lovely.
   She that knew not where to hide,
Is gone again like a jeweled fish from the hand,
   Is lost on every side.

Mute, mute, I make my way to the garden,
   Thither where she last was seen;
The heavy foot of the frost is on the flags there,
   Where her light step has been.

Gone, gone again is Summer the lovely,
   Gone again on every side,
Lost again like a shining fish from the hand
   Into the shadowy tide.

To the Wife of a Sick Friend

Shelter this candle from the wind.
Hold it steady. In its light
The cave wherein we wander lost
Glitters with frosty stalactite,
Blossoms with mineral rose and lotus,
Sparkles with crystal moon and star,
Till a man would rather be lost than found:
We have forgotten where we are.

Shelter this candle. Shrewdly blowing
Down the cave from a secret door
Enters our only foe, the wind.
Hold it steady. Lest we stand,
Each in a sudden, separate dark,
The hot wax spattered upon your hand,
The smoking wick in my nostrils strong,
The inner eyelid red and green
For a moment yet with moons and roses,—
Then the unmitigated dark.

Alone, alone, in a terrible place,
In utter dark without a face,
With only the dripping of the water on the stone,
And the sound of your tears, and the taste of my
    own.

The Bobolink

Black bird scudding
Under the rainy sky,
How wet your wings must be!
And your small head how sleek and cold with water.

Oh, Bobolink, 'tis you!
Over the buffeted orchard in the summer draught,
Chuckling and singing, charging the rainy cloud,
A little bird gone daft,
A little bird with a secret.

Only the bobolink on the rainy
Rhubarb blossom,
Knows my heart. . . .
For whom adversity has not a word to say that can be
    heard
Above the din of summer.
The rain has taught us nothing. And the hooves of
    cattle, and the cat in the grass
Have taught us nothing.
The hawk that motionless above the hill
In the pure sky
Stands like a blackened planet
Has taught us nothing,—seeing him shut his wings and
    fall
Has taught us nothing at all.
In the shadow of the hawk we feather our nests.

Bobolink, you and I, an airy fool and an earthy,
Chuckling under the rain!

I shall never be sad again.
I shall never be sad again.

Ah, sweet, absurd,
Belovèd, bedraggled bird!

The Hawkweed

Between the red-top and the rye,
  Between the buckwheat and the corn,
The ploughman sees with sullen eye
The hawkweed licking at the sky:

  Three level acres all forlorn,
  Unfertile, sour, outrun, outworn,
  Free as the day that they were born.

Southward and northward, west and east,
  The sulphate and the lime are spread;
Harrowed and sweetened, urged, increased,
The furrow sprouts for man and beast:

  While of the hawkweed's radiant head
  No stanchion reeks, no stock is fed.

Triumphant up the taken field
    The tractor and the plough advance;
Blest be the healthy germ concealed
In the rich earth, and blest the yield:

    And blest be Beauty, that enchants
    The frail, the solitary lance.

To a Friend Estranged from Me

Now goes under, and I watch it go under, the sun
That will not rise again.
Today has seen the setting, in your eyes cold and sense-
    less as the sea,
Of friendship better than bread, and of bright charity
That lifts a man a little above the beasts that run.

That this could be!
That I should live to see
Most vulgar Pride, that stale obstreperous clown,
So fitted out with purple robe and crown
To stand among his betters! Face to face
With outraged me in this once holy place,
Where Wisdom was a favoured guest and hunted
    Truth was harboured out of danger,
He bulks enthroned, a lewd, an insupportable
    stranger!

I would have sworn, indeed I swore it:
The hills may shift, the waters may decline,
Winter may twist the stem from the twig that bore it,
But never your love from me, your hand from mine.

Now goes under the sun, and I watch it go under.
Farewell, sweet light, great wonder!
You, too, farewell,—but fare not well enough to
    dream
You have done wisely to invite the night before the
    darkness came.

The Road to Avrillé

April again in Avrillé,
    And the brown lark in air.
And you and I a world apart,
    That walked together there.

The cuckoo spoke from out the wood,
    The lark from out the sky.
Embraced upon the highway stood
    Love sick you and I.

The rosy peasant left his bees,
  The carrier slowed his cart,
To shout us blithe obscenities,
  And bless us from the heart,

Who long before the year was out,
  Under the autumn rain,
Far from the road to Avrillé,
  Parted with little pain.

For Pao-Chin, a Boatman on the Yellow Sea

Where is he now, in his soiled shirt reeking of garlic,
Sculling his sampan home, and night approaching
    fast—
The red sail hanging wrinkled on the bamboo mast;
Where is he now, I shall remember my whole life long
With love and praise, for the sake of a small song
Played on a Chinese flute?
                          I have been sad;
I have been in cities where the song was all I had,—
A treasure never to be bartered by the hungry days.

Where is he now, for whom I carry in my heart
This love, this praise?

Northern April

O mind, beset by music never for a moment quiet,—
The wind at the flue, the wind strumming the shutter;
The soft, antiphonal speech of the doubled brook,
    never for a moment quiet;
The rush of the rain against the glass, his voice in the
    eaves-gutter!

Where shall I lay you to sleep, and the robins be
    quiet?
Lay you to sleep—and the frogs be silent in the
    marsh?
Crashes the sleet from the bough and the bough sighs
    upward, never for a moment quiet.
April is upon us, pitiless and young and harsh.

O April, full of blood, full of breath, have pity upon
    us!
Pale, where the winter like a stone has been lifted
    away, we emerge like yellow grass.
Be for a moment quiet, buffet us not, have pity upon
    us,
Till the green come back into the vein, till the gid-
    diness pass.

There at Dusk I Found You

There at dusk I found you, walking and weeping
Upon the broken flags,
Where at dusk the dumb white nicotine awakes and
utters her fragrance
In a garden sleeping.

Looking askance you said:
Love is dead.

Under our eyes without warning softly the summer
afternoon let fall
The rose upon the wall,
And it lay there splintered.
Terribly then into my heart the forgotten anguish
entered.

I saw the dark stone on the smallest finger of your
hand,
And the clean cuff above.
No more, no more the dark stone on the smallest
finger
Of your brown and naked arm,
Lifting my body in love!

Worse than dead is he of the wounded wing,
Who walks between us, weeping upon the cold flags,
Bleeding and weeping, dragging his broken wing.
He has gathered the rose into his hand and chafed her
    with his breath.
But the rose is quiet and pale. She has forgotten us
    all.
Even spring.
Even death.

As for me, I have forgotten nothing,—nor shall I ever
    forget—
But this one thing:
I have forgotten which of us it was
That hurt his wing.
I only know his limping flight above us in the blue air
Toward the sunset cloud
Is more than I can bear.

You, you there,
Stiff-necked and angry, holding up your head so
    proud,
Have you not seen how pitiful lame he flies, and none
    to befriend him?
Speak! Are you blind? Are you dead?
Shall we call him back? Shall we mend him?

Being Young and Green

Being young and green, I said in love's despite:
Never in the world will I to living wight
Give over, air my mind
To anyone,
Hang out its ancient secrets in the strong wind
To be shredded and faded. . . .

Oh, me, invaded
And sacked by the wind and the sun!

Mist in the Valley

These hills, to hurt me more,
That am hurt already enough,—
Having left the sea behind,
Having turned suddenly and left the shore
That I had loved beyond all words, even a song's
    words, to convey,

And built me a house on upland acres,
Sweet with the pinxter, bright and rough
With the rusty blackbird long before the winter's
    done,
But smelling never of bayberry hot in the sun,
Nor ever loud with the pounding of the long white
    breakers,—

These hills, beneath the October moon,
Sit in the valley white with mist
Like islands in a quiet bay,

Jut out from shore into the mist,
Wooded with poplar dark as pine,
Like points of land into a quiet bay.

(Just in that way
The harbour met the bay)

Stricken too sore for tears,
I stand, remembering the islands and the sea's lost
    sound. . . .
Life at its best no longer than the sand-peep's cry,
And I two years, two years,
Tilling an upland ground!

The Hardy Garden

Now let forever the phlox and the rose be tended
Here where the rain has darkened and the sun has
    dried
So many times the terrace, yet is love unended,
    Love has not died.

Let here no seed of a season, that the winter
But once assails, take root and for a time endure;
But only such as harbour at the frozen centre
  The germ secure.

Set here the phlox and the iris, and establish
Pink and valerian, and the great and lesser bells;
But suffer not the sisters of the year, to publish
  That frost prevails.

How far from home in a world of mortal burdens
Is Love, that may not die, and is forever young!
Set roses here: surround her only with such maidens
  As speak her tongue.

The Pigeons

Well I remember the pigeons in the sunny arbour
Beyond your open door;
How they conversed throughout the afternoon in
    their monotonous voices never for a moment
    still;
Always of yesterday they spoke, and of the days
    before,
Rustling the vine-leaves, twitching the dark shadows
    of the leaves on the bright sill.

You said, the soft curring and droning of the pigeons
    in the vine
Was a pretty thing enough to the passer-by,
But a maddening thing to a man with his head in his
    hands,—"Like mine! Like mine!"
You said, and ran to the door and waved them off into
    the sky.

They did not come back. The arbour was empty of
    their cooing.
The shadows of the leaves were still. "Whither have
    they flown, then?"
I said, and waited for their wings, but they did not
    come back. If I had known then
What I know now, I never would have left your door.

Tall in your faded smock, with steady hand
Mingling the brilliant pigments, painting your inter-
    secting planes you stand,
In a quiet room, empty of the past, of its droning and
    cooing,
Thinking I know not what, but thinking of me no
    more,
That left you with a light word, that loving and
    ruing
Walk in the streets of a city you have never seen,
Walk in a noise of yesterday and of the days before,
Walk in a cloud of wings intolerable, shutting out the
    sun as if it never had been.

The Buck in the Snow

White sky, over the hemlocks bowed with snow,
Saw you not at the beginning of evening the antlered
    buck and his doe
Standing in the apple-orchard? I saw them. I saw them
    suddenly go,
Tails up, with long leaps lovely and slow,
Over the stone-wall into the wood of hemlocks bowed
    with snow.

Now lies he here, his wild blood scalding the snow.

How strange a thing is death, bringing to his knees,
    bringing to his antlers
The buck in the snow.
How strange a thing,—a mile away by now, it may be,
Under the heavy hemlocks that as the moments pass
Shift their loads a little, letting fall a feather of
    snow—
Life, looking out attentive from the eyes of the doe.

The Anguish

I would to God I were quenched and fed
As in my youth
From the flask of song, and the good bread
Of beauty richer than truth.

The anguish of the world is on my tongue.
My bowl is filled to the brim with it; there is more
    than I can eat.
Happy are the toothless old and the toothless young,
That cannot rend this meat.

Justice Denied in Massachusetts

Let us abandon then our gardens and go home
And sit in the sitting-room.
Shall the larkspur blossom or the corn grow under this
    cloud?
Sour to the fruitful seed
Is the cold earth under this cloud,
Fostering quack and weed, we have marched upon but
    cannot conquer;
We have bent the blades of our hoes against the stalks
    of them.

Let us go home, and sit in the sitting-room.
Not in our day
Shall the cloud go over and the sun rise as before,
Beneficent upon us
Out of the glittering bay,
And the warm winds be blown inward from the sea
Moving the blades of corn
With a peaceful sound.

Forlorn, forlorn,
Stands the blue hay-rack by the empty mow.
And the petals drop to the ground,
Leaving the tree unfruited.
The sun that warmed our stooping backs and withered
      the weed uprooted—
We shall not feel it again.
We shall die in darkness, and be buried in the rain.

What from the splendid dead
We have inherited—
Furrows sweet to the grain, and the weed subdued—
See now the slug and the mildew plunder.
Evil does overwhelm
The larkspur and the corn;
We have seen them go under.

Let us sit here, sit still,
Here in the sitting-room until we die;
At the step of Death on the walk, rise and go;
Leaving to our children's children this beautiful door-
      way,
And this elm,
And a blighted earth to till
With a broken hoe.

Hangman's Oak

Before the cock in the barnyard spoke,
    Before it well was day,
Horror like a serpent from about the Hangman's Oak
    Uncoiled and slid away.

Pity and Peace were on the limb
    That bore such bitter fruit.
Deep he lies, and the desperate blood of him
    Befriends the innocent root.

Brother, I said to the air beneath the bough
    Whence he had swung,
It will not be long for any of us now;
    We do not grow young.

It will not be long for the knotter of ropes, not long
    For the sheriff or for me,
Or for any of them that came five hundred strong
    To see you swing from a tree.

Side by side together in the belly of Death
    We sit without hope,
You, and I, and the mother that gave you breath,
    And the tree, and the rope.

Wine from These Grapes

Wine from these grapes I shall be treading surely
Morning and noon and night until I die.
Stained with these grapes I shall lie down to die.

If you would speak with me on any matter,
At any time, come where these grapes are grown;
And you will find me treading them to must.
Lean then above me sagely, lest I spatter
Drops of the wine I tread from grapes and dust.

Stained with these grapes I shall lie down to die.
Three women come to wash me clean
Shall not erase this stain.
Nor leave me lying purely,
Awaiting the black lover.
Death, fumbling to uncover
My body in his bed,
Shall know
There has been one
Before him.

To Those Without Pity

Cruel of heart, lay down my song.
Your reading eyes have done me wrong.
Not for you was the pen bitten,
And the mind wrung, and the song written.

Dawn

All men are lonely now.
This is the hour when no man has a friend.
Memory and Faith suspend
From their spread wings above a cool abyss.
All friendships end.

He that lay awake
All night
For sweet love's unregenerate sake,
Sleeps in the grey light.

The lover, if he dream at all,
Dreams not of her whose languid hand sleeps open at
    his side;
He is gone to another bride.
And she he leaves behind
Sighs not in sleep "Unkind . . . unkind . . .";
She walks in a garden of yellow quinces;
Smiling, she gathers yellow quinces in a basket
Of willow and laurel combined.

Should I return to your door,
Fresh and haggard out of the morning air,
There would be darkness on the stair,
And a dead close odor painfully sad,
That was not there before.
There would be silence. There would be heavy steps
    across the floor.
And you would let me in, frowning with sleep
Under your rumpled hair.

Beautiful now upon the ear unshut by slumber
The rich and varied voices of the waking day!—
The mighty, mournful whistles without number
Of tugs and ferries, mingling, confounding, failing,
Thinning to separate notes of wailing,
Making stupendous music on the misty bay.

Now through the echoing street in the growing light,
Intent on errands that the sun approves,
Clatter unashamed the heavy wheels and hooves
Before the silent houses; briskly they say:
"Marshal not me among the enterprises of the night.
I am the beginning of the day."

To a Young Girl

Shall I despise you that your colourless tears
Made rainbows in your lashes, and you forgot to weep?
Would we were half so wise, that eke a grief out
By sitting in the dark, until we fall asleep.

I only fear lest, being by nature sunny,
By and by you will weep no more at all,
And fall asleep in the light, having lost with the
    tears
The colour in the lashes that comes as the tears fall.

I would not have you darken your lids with weeping,
Beautiful eyes, but I would have you weep enough
To wet the fingers of the hand held over the eye-lids,
And stain a little the light frock's delicate stuff.

For there came into my mind, as I watched you wink-
    ing the tears down,
Laughing faces, blown from the west and the east,
Faces lovely and proud that I have prized and cher-
    ished;
Nor were the loveliest among them those that had
    wept the least.

Evening on Lesbos

Twice having seen your shingled heads adorable
Side by side, the onyx and the gold,
I know that I have had what I could not hold.

Twice have I entered the room, not knowing she was
    here.
Two agate eyes, two eyes of malachite,
Twice have been turned upon me, hard and bright.

Whereby I know my loss.
                   Oh, not restorable
Sweet incense, mounting in the windless night!

Dirge Without Music

I am not resigned to the shutting away of loving hearts
    in the hard ground.
So it is, and so it will be, for so it has been, time out
    of mind:
Into the darkness they go, the wise and the lovely.
    Crowned with lilies and with laurel they go; but
    I am not resigned.

Lovers and thinkers, into the earth with you.
Be one with the dull, the indiscriminate dust.
A fragment of what you felt, of what you knew,
A formula, a phrase remains,—but the best is lost.

The answers quick and keen, the honest look, the
    laughter, the love,—
They are gone. They are gone to feed the roses.
    Elegant and curled
Is the blossom. Fragrant is the blossom. I know. But I
    do not approve.
More precious was the light in your eyes than all the
    roses in the world.

Down, down, down into the darkness of the grave
Gently they go, the beautiful, the tender, the kind;
Quietly they go, the intelligent, the witty, the brave.
I know. But I do not approve. And I am not resigned.

Memory of Cassis

Do you recall how we sat by the smokily-burning
Twisted odorous trunk of the olive-tree,
In the inn on the cliff, and skinned the ripe green
figs,
And heard the white sirocco driving in the sea?

The thunder and the smother there where like a ship's
prow
The lighthouse breasted the wave? how wanly through
the wild spray
Under our peering eyes the eye of the light looked out,
Disheveled, but without dismay?

Do you recall the sweet-alyssum over the ledges
Crawling and the tall heather and the mushrooms
under the pines,
And the deep white dust of the broad road leading
outward
To a world forgotten, between the dusty almonds and
the dusty vines?

Portrait

Over and over I have heard,
As now I hear it,
Your voice harsh and light as the scratching of dry
     leaves over the hard ground,
Your voice forever assailed and shaken by the wind
     from the island
Of illustrious living and dead, that never dies down,
And bending at moments under the terrible weight of
     the perfect word,
Here in this room without fire, without comfort of any
     kind,
Reading aloud to me immortal page after page con-
     ceived in a mortal mind.
Beauty at such moments before me like a wild bright
     bird
Has been in the room, and eyed me, and let me come
     near it.

I could not ever nor can I to this day
Acquaint you with the triumph and the sweet rest
These hours have brought to me and always bring,—
Rapture, coloured like the wild bird's neck and wing,
Comfort, softer than the feathers of its breast.

Always, and even now, when I rise to go,
Your eyes blaze out from a face gone wickedly pale;
I try to tell you what I would have you know,—
What peace it was; you cry me down; you scourge me
     with a salty flail;
You will not have it so.

Winter Night

Pile high the hickory and the light
Log of chestnut struck by the blight.
Welcome-in the winter night.

The day has gone in hewing and felling,
Sawing and drawing wood to the dwelling
For the night of talk and story-telling.

These are the hours that give the edge
To the blunted axe and the bent wedge,
Straighten the saw and lighten the sledge.

Here are question and reply,
And the fire reflected in the thinking eye.
So peace, and let the bob-cat cry.

The Cameo

Forever over now, forever, forever gone
That day. Clear and diminished like a scene
Carven in cameo, the lighthouse, and the cove be-
    tween
The sandy cliffs, and the boat drawn up on the beach;
And the long skirt of a lady innocent and young,
Her hand resting on her bosom, her head hung;
And the figure of a man in earnest speech.

Clear and diminished like a scene cut in cameo
The lighthouse, and the boat on the beach, and the
    two shapes
Of the woman and the man; lost like the lost day
Are the words that passed, and the pain,—discarded,
    cut away
From the stone, as from the memory the heat of the
    tears escapes.

O troubled forms, O early love unfortunate and
    hard,
Time has estranged you into a jewel cold and pure;
From the action of the waves and from the action of
    sorrow forever secure,
White against a ruddy cliff you stand, chalcedony on
    sard.

Counting-out Rhyme

Silver bark of beech, and sallow
Bark of yellow birch and yellow
    Twig of willow.

Stripe of green in moosewood maple,
Colour seen in leaf of apple,
  Bark of popple.

Wood of popple pale as moonbeam,
Wood of oak for yoke and barn-beam,
  Wood of hornbeam.

Silver bark of beech, and hollow
Stem of elder, tall and yellow
  Twig of willow.

The Plum Gatherer

The angry nettle and the mild
  Grew together under the blue-plum trees.
I could not tell as a child
  Which was my friend of these.

Always the angry nettle in the skirt of his sister
  Caught my wrist that reached over the ground,
Where alike I gathered,—for the one was sweet and the
    other wore a frosty dust—
  The broken plum and the sound.

The plum-trees are barren now and the black knot is
  upon them,
  That stood so white in the spring.
I would give, to recall the sweetness and the frost of
  the lost blue plums,
  Anything, anything.
I thrust my arm among the grey ambiguous nettles,
  and wait.
  But they do not sting.

West Country Song

Sun came up, bigger than all my sorrow;
Lark in air so high, and his song clean through me.
Now comes night, hushing the lark in's furrow,
  And the rain falls fine.
What have I done with what was dearest to me?

Thatch and wick, fagot, and tea on trivet,—
These and more it was; it was all my cheer.
Now comes night, smelling of box and privet,
  And the rain falls fine.
Have I left it out in the rain?—It is not here.

Pueblo Pot

There as I bent above the broken pot from the mesa
    pueblo,
Mournfully many times its patterned shards piecing
    together and laying aside,
Appeared upon the house-top, two Navajos enchanted,
    the red-shafted flicker and his bride,
And stepped with lovely stride
To the pergola, flashing the wonder of their under-
    wings;
There stood, mysterious and harsh and sleek,
Wrenching the indigo berry from the shedding wood-
    bine with strong ebony beak.

His head without a crest
Wore the red full moon for crown;
The black new moon was crescent on the breast of
    each;
From the bodies of both a visible heat beat down,
And from the motion of their necks a shadow would
    fly and fall,
Skimming the court and in the yellow adobe wall
Cleaving a blue breach.

Powerful was the beauty of these birds.
It boomed like a struck bell in the silence deep and
    hot.
I stooped above the shattered clay; passionately I cried
    to the beauty of these birds,
"Solace the broken pot!"

The beauty of these birds
Opened its lips to speak;
Colours were its words,
The scarlet shaft on the grey cheek,
The purple berry in the ebony beak.
It said, "I cannot console
The broken thing; I can only make it whole."

Wisdom, heretic flower, I was ever afraid
Of your large, cool petals without scent!
Shocked, betrayed,
I turned to the comfort of grief, I bent
Above the lovely shards.
But their colours had faded in the fierce light of the
    birds.
And as for the birds, they were gone. As suddenly as
    they had come, they went.

When Caesar Fell

When Caesar fell, where yellow Tiber rolls
   Its heavy waters muddy,
Life, that was ebbing from a hundred holes
   In Caesar's body,
Cried with a hundred voices to the common air,
   The unimperial day,
"Gather me up, oh, pour me into the veins of even a
     gilder of hair!
   Let me not vanish away!"

The teeth of Caesar at the ignoble word
   Were ground together in pride;
No sound came from his lips: the world has heard
   How Caesar died.
In the Roman dust the cry of Caesar's blood
   Was heard and heard without wonder
Only by the fly that swam in the red flood
   Till his head went under.

Lethe

   Ah, drink again
   This river that is the taker-away of pain,
   And the giver-back of beauty!

In these cool waves
What can be lost?—
Only the sorry cost
Of the lovely thing, ah, never the thing itself!

The level flood that laves
The hot brow
And the stiff shoulder
Is at our temples now.

Gone is the fever,
But not into the river;
Melted the frozen pride,
But the tranquil tide
Runs never the warmer for this,
Never the colder.

Immerse the dream.
Drench the kiss.
Dip the song in the stream.

On First Having Heard the Skylark

Not knowing he rose from earth, not having seen him
rise,
Not knowing the fallow furrow was his home,
And that high wing, untouchable, untainted,

A wing of earth, with the warm loam
Closely acquainted,
I shuddered at his cry and caught my heart.
Relentless out of heaven his sweet crying like a crystal
dart
Was launched against me. Scanning the empty sky
I stood with thrown-back head until the world reeled.
Still, still he sped his unappeasable shafts against my
breast without a shield.
He cried forever from his unseen throat
Between me and the sun.
He would not end his singing, he would not have
done.
"Serene and pitiless note, whence, whence are you?"
I cried. "Alas, these arrows, how fast they fall!
Ay, me, beset by angels in unequal fight,
Alone high on the shaven down surprised, and not a
tree in sight!"

Even as I spoke he was revealed
Above me in the bright air,
A dark articulate atom in the mute enormous blue,
A mortal bird, flying and singing in the morning there.
Even as I spoke I spied him, and I knew,
And called him by his name;
"Blithe Spirit!" I cried. Transfixed by more than
mortal spears
I fell; I lay among the foreign daisies pink and small,
And wept, staining their innocent faces with fast-
flowing tears.

To a Musician

Who, now, when evening darkens the water and the
    stream is dull,
Slowly, in a delicate frock, with her leghorn hat in her
    hand,
At your side from under the golden osiers moves,
Faintly smiling, shattered by the charm of your
    voice?

There, today, as in the days when I knew you well,
The willow sheds upon the stream its narrow leaves,
And the quiet flowing of the water and its faint smell
Are balm to the heart that grieves.

Together with the sharp discomfort of loving you,
Ineffable you, so lovely and so aloof,
There is laid upon the spirit the calmness of the river
    view:
Together they fall, the pain and its reproof.

Who, now, under the yellow willows at the water's
    edge
Closes defeated lips upon the trivial word unspoken,
And lifts her soft eyes freighted with a heavy pledge
To your eyes empty of pledges, even of pledges
    broken?

From *POEMS SELECTED FOR YOUNG PEOPLE*

From a Very Little Sphinx

I

Come along in then, little girl!
Or else stay out!
But in the open door she stands,
And bites her lip and twists her hands,
And stares upon me, trouble-eyed:
"Mother," she says, "I can't decide!
I can't decide!"

II

Oh, burdock, and you other dock,
That have ground coffee for your seeds,
And lovely long thin daisies, dear—
She said that you are weeds!
She said, "Oh, what a fine bouquet!"
But afterwards I heard her say,
"She's always dragging in those weeds."

III

Everybody but just me
Despises burdocks. Mother, she
Despises 'em the most because
They stick so to my socks and drawers.
But father, when he sits on some,
Can't speak a decent word for 'em.

IV

I know a hundred ways to die.
I've often thought I'd try one:
Lie down beneath a motor truck
Some day when standing by one.

Or throw myself from off a bridge—
Except such things must be
So hard upon the scavengers
And men that clean the sea.

I know some poison I could drink.
I've often thought I'd taste it.
But mother bought it for the sink,
And drinking it would waste it.

V

Look, Edwin! Do you see that boy
Talking to the other boy?
No, over there by those two men—
Wait, don't look now—now look again.
No, not the one in navy-blue;
That's the one he's talking to.
Sure you see him? Stripèd pants?
Well, *he was born in Paris, France.*

VI

All the grown-up people say,
"What, those ugly thistles?
Mustn't touch them! Keep away!
Prickly! Full of bristles!"

Yet they never make me bleed
Half so much as roses!
Must be purple is a weed,
And pink and white is posies.

Wonder where this horseshoe went.
Up and down, up and down,
Up and past the monument,
Maybe into town.

Wait a minute. "Horseshoe,
How far have you been?"
Says it's been to Salem
And halfway to Lynn.

Wonder who was in the team.
Wonder what they saw.
Wonder if they passed a bridge—
Bridge with a draw.

Says it went from one bridge
Straight upon another.
Says it took a little girl
Driving with her mother.

From *WINE FROM THESE GRAPES*

The Return

Earth does not understand her child,
  Who from the loud gregarious town
Returns, depleted and defiled,
  To the still woods, to fling him down.

Earth can not count the sons she bore:
  The wounded lynx, the wounded man
Come trailing blood unto her door;
  She shelters both as best she can.

But she is early up and out,
  To trim the year or strip its bones;
She has no time to stand about
  Talking of him in undertones

Who has no aim but to forget,
  Be left in peace, be lying thus
For days, for years, for centuries yet,
  Unshaven and anonymous;

Who, marked for failure, dulled by grief,
  Has traded in his wife and friend
For this warm ledge, this alder leaf:
  Comfort that does not comprehend.

October—An Etching

There where the woodcock his long bill among the
    alders
Forward in level flight propels,
Tussocks of faded grass are islands in the pasture
    swamp
Where the small foot, if it be light as well, can pass
Dry-shod to rising ground.

Not so the boot of the hunter.
Chilly and black and halfway to the knee
Is the thick water there, heavy wading,
Uneven to the step; there the more cautious ones,
Pausing for a moment, break their guns.
There the white setter ticked with black
Sets forth with silky feathers on the bird's track
And wet to his pink skin and half his size comes
    back.

Cows are pastured there; they have made a path among
    the alders.
By now the keeper's boy has found
The chalk of the woodcock on the trampled ground.

Autumn Daybreak

Cold wind of autumn, blowing loud
At dawn, a fortnight overdue,
Jostling the doors, and tearing through
My bedroom to rejoin the cloud,

I know—for I can hear the hiss
And scrape of leaves along the floor—
How many boughs, lashed bare by this,
Will rake the cluttered sky once more.

Tardy, and somewhat south of east,
The sun will rise at length, made known
More by the meagre light increased
Than by a disk in splendour shown;

When, having but to turn my head,
Through the stripped maple I shall see,
Bleak and remembered, patched with red,
The hill all summer hid from me.

The Oak-Leaves

Yet in the end, defeated too, worn out and ready to
    fall,
Hangs from the drowsy tree with cramped and des-
    perate stem above the ditch the last leaf of all.

There is something to be learned, I guess, from look-
    ing at the dead leaves under the living tree;
Something to be set to a lusty tune and learned and
    sung, it well might be;
Something to be learned—though I was ever a ten-
    o'clock scholar at this school—
Even perhaps by me.

But my heart goes out to the oak-leaves that are the
    last to sigh
"Enough," and loose their hold;
They have boasted to the nudging frost and to the two-
    and-thirty winds that they would never die,
Never even grow old.
(These are those russet leaves that cling
All winter, even into the spring,
To the dormant bough, in the wood knee-deep in snow
    the only coloured thing.

The Fledgling

So, art thou feathered, art thou flown,
Thou naked thing?—and canst alone
Upon the unsolid summer air
Sustain thyself, and prosper there?

Shall I no more with anxious note
Advise thee through the happy day,
Thrusting the worm into thy throat,
Bearing thine excrement away?

Alas, I think I see thee yet,
Perched on the windy parapet,
Defer thy flight a moment still
To clean thy wing with careful bill.

And thou art feathered, thou art flown;
And hast a project of thine own.

The Hedge of Hemlocks

Somebody long ago
Set out this hedge of hemlocks; brought from the
    woods, I'd say,
Saplings ten inches tall, curving and delicate, not
    shaped like trees,
And set them out, to shut the marshes from the lawn,
A hedge of ferns.

Four feet apart he set them, far apart, leaving them
    room to grow . . .
Whose crowded lower boughs these fifty years at
    least
Are spiky stumps outthrust in all directions, dry,
    dropping scaly bark, in the deep shade making a
    thick
Dust which here and there floats in a short dazzling
    beam.

Green tops, delicate and curving yet, above this fence
    of brush, like ferns,
You have done well: more than the marshes now is
    shut away from his protected dooryard;
The mountain, too, is shut away; not even the wind
May trespass here to stir the purple phlox in the tall
    grass.

And yet how easily one afternoon between
Your stems, unheard, snapping no twig, dislodging no
    shell of loosened bark, unseen
Even by the spider through whose finished web he
    walked, and left it as he found it,
A neighbour entered.

Cap D'Antibes

The storm is over, and the land has forgotten the
    storm; the trees are still.
Under this sun the rain dries quickly.
Cones from the sea-pines cover the ground again
Where yesterday for my fire I gathered all in sight;
But the leaves are meek. The smell of the small
    alyssum that grows wild here
Is in the air. It is a childish morning.

More sea than land am I; my sulky mind, whipped
    high by tempest in the night, is not so soon
    appeased.
Into my occupations with dull roar
It washes,
It recedes.
Even as at my side in the calm day the disturbed Medi-
    terranean
Lurches with heavy swell against the bird-twittering
    shore.

From a Train Window

Precious in the light of the early sun the Housatonic
Between its not unscalable mountains flows.
Precious in the January morning the shabby fur of the
    cat-tails by the stream.
The farmer driving his horse to the feed-store for a
    sack of cracked corn
Is not in haste; there is no whip in the socket.

Pleasant enough, gay even, by no means sad
Is the rickety graveyard on the hill. Those are not
    cypress trees
Perpendicular among the lurching slabs, but cedars
    from the neighbourhood,
Native to this rocky land, self-sown. Precious
In the early light, reassuring
Is the grave-scarred hillside.
As if after all, the earth might know what it is about.

The Fawn

There it was I saw what I shall never forget
And never retrieve.
Monstrous and beautiful to human eyes, hard to be-
    lieve,
He lay, yet there he lay,
Asleep on the moss, his head on his polished cleft
    small ebony hooves,
The child of the doe, the dappled child of the deer.

Surely his mother had never said, "Lie here
Till I return," so spotty and plain to see
On the green moss lay he.
His eyes had opened; he considered me.

I would have given more than I care to say
To thrifty ears, might I have had him for my friend
One moment only of that forest day:

Might I have had the acceptance, not the love
Of those clear eyes;
Might I have been for him the bough above
Or the root beneath his forest bed,
A part of the forest, seen without surprise.

Was it alarm, or was it the wind of my fear lest he
    depart
That jerked him to his jointy knees,
And sent him crashing off, leaping and stumbling
On his new legs, between the stems of the white trees?

Valentine

Oh, what a shining town were Death
Woke you therein, and drew your breath,
My buried love; and all you were,
Caught up and cherished, even there.
Those evil windows loved of none
Would blaze as if they caught the sun.

Woke you in Heaven, Death's kinder name,
And downward in sweet gesture came
From your cold breast your rigid hand,
Then Heaven would be my native land.

But you are nowhere: you are gone
All roads into Oblivion.
Whither I would disperse, till then
From home a banished citizen.

In the Grave No Flower

Here dock and tare.
But there
No flower.

Here beggar-ticks, 'tis true;
Here the rank-smelling
Thorn-apple,—and who
Would plant this by his dwelling?
Here every manner of weed
To mock the faithful harrow:
Thistles, that feed
None but the finches; yarrow,
Blue vervain, yellow charlock; here
Bindweed, that chokes the struggling year;
Broad plantain and narrow.

But there no flower.

The rye is vexed and thinned,
The wheat comes limping home,
By vetch and whiteweed harried, and the sandy bloom
Of the sour-grass; here
Dandelions,—and the wind
Will blow them everywhere.

Save there.
There
No flower.

Childhood Is the Kingdom Where Nobody Dies

Childhood is not from birth to a certain age and at a
    certain age
The child is grown, and puts away childish things.
Childhood is the kingdom where nobody dies.

Nobody that matters, that is. Distant relatives of
    course
Die, whom one never has seen or has seen for an
    hour,
And they gave one candy in a pink-and-green stripèd
    bag, or a jack-knife,
And went away, and cannot really be said to have lived
    at all.

And cats die. They lie on the floor and lash their
    tails,
And their reticent fur is suddenly all in motion
With fleas that one never knew were there,
Polished and brown, knowing all there is to know,
Trekking off into the living world.
You fetch a shoe-box, but it's much too small, because
    she won't curl up now:
So you find a bigger box, and bury her in the yard,
    and weep.

But you do not wake up a month from then, two
    months,
A year from then, two years, in the middle of the
    night
And weep, with your knuckles in your mouth, and say
    Oh, God! Oh, God!
Childhood is the kingdom where nobody dies that
    matters,—mothers and fathers don't die.

And if you have said, "For heaven's sake, must you al-
    ways be kissing a person?"
Or, "I do wish to gracious you'd stop tapping on the
    window with your thimble!"
Tomorrow, or even the day after tomorrow if you're
    busy having fun,
Is plenty of time to say, "I'm sorry, mother."

To be grown up is to sit at the table with people who
    have died, who neither listen nor speak;
Who do not drink their tea, though they always said
Tea was such a comfort.

Run down into the cellar and bring up the last jar of
    raspberries; they are not tempted.
Flatter them, ask them what was it they said exactly
That time, to the bishop, or to the overseer, or to Mrs.
    Mason;
They are not taken in.
Shout at them, get red in the face, rise,
Drag them up out of their chairs by their stiff shoul-
    ders and shake them and yell at them;

They are not startled, they are not even embarrassed;
    they slide back into their chairs.

Your tea is cold now.
You drink it standing up,
And leave the house.

IV

The Solid Sprite Who Stands Alone

The solid sprite who stands alone,
    And walks the world with equal stride,
Grieve though he may, is not undone
    Because a friend has died.

He knows that man is born to care,
    And ten and threescore's all his span;
And this is comfort and to spare
    For such a level man.

He is not made like crooked me,
    Who cannot rise nor lift my head,
And all because what had to be
    Has been, what lived is dead;

Who lie among my tears and rust,
    And all because a mortal brain
That loved to think, is clogged with dust,
    And will not think again.

Spring in the Garden

Ah, cannot the curled shoots of the larkspur that you
    loved so,
Cannot the spiny poppy that no winter kills
Instruct you how to return through the thawing
    ground and the thin snow
Into this April sun that is driving the mist between
    the hills?

A good friend to the monkshood in a time of need
You were, and the lupine's friend as well;
But I see the lupine lift the ground like a tough weed
And the earth over the monkshood swell,

And I fear that not a root in all this heaving sea
Of land, has nudged you where you lie, has found
Patience and time to direct you, numb and stupid as
    you still must be
From your first winter underground.

Sonnet

Time, that renews the tissues of this frame,
That built the child and hardened the soft bone,
Taught him to wail, to blink, to walk alone,
Stare, question, wonder, give the world a name,
Forget the watery darkness whence he came,
Attends no less the boy to manhood grown,
Brings him new raiment, strips him of his own:
All skins are shed at length, remorse, even shame.
Such hope is mine, if this indeed be true,
I dread no more the first white in my hair,
Or even age itself, the easy shoe,
The cane, the wrinkled hands, the special chair:
Time, doing this to me, may alter too
My anguish, into something I can bear.

———————

Aubade

Cool and beautiful as the blossom of the wild carrot
With its crimson central eye,
Round and beautiful as the globe of the onion blos-
  som
Were her pale breasts whereon I laid me down to die.

From the wound of my enemy that thrust me through
  in the dark wood
I arose; with sweat on my lip and the wild woodgrasses
  in my spur
I arose and stood.
But never did I arise from loving her.

Sappho Crosses the Dark River into Hades

Charon, indeed, your dreaded oar,
With what a peaceful sound it dips
Into the stream; how gently, too,
From the wet blade the water drips.

I knew a ferryman before.
But he was not so old as you.
He spoke from unembittered lips,

With careless eyes on the bright sea
One day, such bitter words to me
As age and wisdom never knew.

This was a man of meagre fame;
He ferried merchants from the shore
To Mitylene (whence I came)
On Lesbos; Phaon is his name.

I hope that he will never die,
As I have done, and come to dwell
In this pale city we approach.
Not that, indeed, I wish him well,
(Though never have I wished him harm)
But rather that I hope to find
In some unechoing street of Hell
The peace I long have had in mind:
A peace whereon may not encroach
That supple back, the strong brown arm,
That curving mouth, the sunburned curls;
But rather that I would rely,
Having come so far, at such expense,
Upon some quiet lodging whence
I need not hear his voice go by
In scraps of talk with boys and girls.

Epitaph

Grieve not for happy Claudius, he is dead;
And empty is his skull.
Pity no longer, arm-in-arm with Dread,
Walks in that polished hall.

Joy, too, is fled.
But no man can have all.

On Thought in Harness

My falcon to my wrist
Returns
From no high air.
I sent her toward the sun that burns
Above the mist;
But she has not been there.

Her talons are not cold; her beak
Is closed upon no wonder;
Her head stinks of its hood, her feathers reek
Of me, that quake at the thunder.

Degraded bird, I give you back your eyes forever,
    ascend now whither you are tossed;
Forsake this wrist, forsake this rhyme;
Soar, eat ether, see what has never been seen; depart,
    be lost,
But climb.

Desolation Dreamed Of

Desolation dreamed of, though not accomplished,
Set my heart to rocking like a boat in a swell.
To every face I met, I said farewell.

Green rollers breaking white along a clean beach . . .
    when shall I reach that island?
Gladly, O painted nails and shaven arm-pits, would I
    see less of you!
Gladly, gladly would I be far from you for a long time,
    O noise and stench of man!

I said farewell. Nevertheless,
Whom have I quitted?—which of my possessions do I
    propose to leave?
Not one. This feigning to be asleep when wide awake
    is all the loneliness
I shall ever achieve.

The Leaf and the Tree

When will you learn, my self, to be
A dying leaf on a living tree?
Budding, swelling, growing strong,
Wearing green, but not for long,

Drawing sustenance from air,
That other leaves, and you not there,
May bud, and at the autumn's call
Wearing russet, ready to fall?

Has not this trunk a deed to do
Unguessed by small and tremulous you?
Shall not these branches in the end
To wisdom and the truth ascend?
And the great lightning plunging by
Look sidewise with a golden eye
To glimpse a tree so tall and proud
It sheds its leaves upon a cloud?

Here, I think, is the heart's grief:
The tree, no mightier than the leaf,
Makes firm its root and spreads its crown
And stands; but in the end comes down.
That airy top no boy could climb
Is trodden in a little time
By cattle on their way to drink.
The fluttering thoughts a leaf can think,
That hears the wind and waits its turn,
Have taught it all a tree can learn.

Time can make soft that iron wood.
The tallest trunk that ever stood,
In time, without a dream to keep,
Crawls in beside the root to sleep.

On the Wide Heath

On the wide heath at evening overtaken,
  When the fast-reddening sun
Drops, and against the sky the looming bracken
  Waves, and the day is done,

Though no unfriendly nostril snuffs his bone,
  Though English wolves be dead,
The fox abroad on errands of his own,
  The adder gone to bed,

The weary traveler from his aching hip
  Lengthens his long stride;
Though Home be but a humming on his lip,
  No happiness, no pride,

He does not drop him under the yellow whin
  To sleep the darkness through;
Home to the yellow light that shines within
  The kitchen of a loud shrew.

Home over stones and sand, through stagnant water
  He goes, mile after mile
Home to a wordless poaching son and a daughter
  With a disdainful smile,

Home to the worn reproach, the disagreeing,
  The shelter, the stale air; content to be
Pecked at, confined, encroached upon,—it being
  Too lonely, to be free.

Apostrophe to Man

(on reflecting that the world is ready to go to war again)

Detestable race, continue to expunge yourself, die
    out.
Breed faster, crowd, encroach, sing hymns, build bomb-
    ing airplanes;
Make speeches, unveil statues, issue bonds, parade;
Convert again into explosives the bewildered ammonia
    and the distracted cellulose;
Convert again into putrescent matter drawing flies
The hopeful bodies of the young; exhort,
Pray, pull long faces, be earnest, be all but overcome,
    be photographed;
Confer, perfect your formulae, commercialize
Bacteria harmful to human tissue,
Put death on the market;
Breed, crowd, encroach, expand, expunge yourself, die
    out,
Homo called *sapiens.*

My Spirit, Sore from Marching

My spirit, sore from marching
    Toward that receding west
Where Pity shall be governor,
    With Wisdom for his guest:

Lie down beside these waters
    That bubble from the spring;

Hear in the desert silence
    The desert sparrow sing;

Draw from the shapeless moment
    Such pattern as you can;
And cleave henceforth to Beauty;
    Expect no more from man.

Man, with his ready answer,
    His sad and hearty word,
For every cause in limbo,
    For every debt deferred,

For every pledge forgotten,
    His eloquent and grim
Deep empty gaze upon you,—
    Expect no more from him.

From cool and aimless Beauty
    Your bread and comfort take,
Beauty, that made no promise,
    And has no word to break;

Have eyes for Beauty only,
    That has no eyes for you;
Follow her struck pavilion,
    Halt with her retinue;

Catch from the board of Beauty
    Such careless crumbs as fall.
Here's hope for priest and layman;
    Here's heresy for all.

Conscientious Objector

I shall die, but that is all that I shall do for Death.

I hear him leading his horse out of the stall; I hear the
    clatter on the barn-floor.
He is in haste; he has business in Cuba, business in the
    Balkans, many calls to make this morning.
But I will not hold the bridle while he cinches the
    girth.
And he may mount by himself: I will not give him a
    leg up.

Though he flick my shoulders with his whip, I will not
    tell him which way the fox ran.
With his hoof on my breast, I will not tell him where
    the black boy hides in the swamp.
I shall die, but that is all that I shall do for Death; I
    am not on his pay-roll.

I will not tell him the whereabouts of my friends nor
    of my enemies either.
Though he promise me much, I will not map him the
    route to any man's door.
Am I a spy in the land of the living, that I should de-
    liver men to Death?
Brother, the password and the plans of our city are
    safe with me; never through me
Shall you be overcome.

Above These Cares

Above these cares my spirit in calm abiding
Floats like a swimmer at sunrise, facing the pale sky;
Peaceful, heaved by the light infrequent lurch of the
    heavy wave serenely sliding
Under his weightless body, aware of the wide morning,
    aware of the gull on the red buoy bedaubed with
    guano, aware of his sharp cry;
Idly athirst for the sea, as who should say:
In a moment I will roll upon my mouth and drink it
    dry.

Painfully, under the pressure that obtains
At the sea's bottom, crushing my lungs and my
    brains
(For the body makes shift to breathe and after a
    fashion flourish
Ten fathoms deep in care,
Ten fathoms down in an element denser than air
Wherein the soul must perish)
I trap and harvest, stilling my stomach's needs;
I crawl forever, hoping never to see
Above my head the limbs of my spirit no longer free
Kicking in frenzy, a swimmer enmeshed in weeds.

If Still Your Orchards Bear

Brother, that breathe the August air
    Ten thousand years from now,
And smell—if still your orchards bear
    Tart apples on the bough—

The early windfall under the tree,
    And see the red fruit shine,
I cannot think your thoughts will be
    Much different from mine.

Should at that moment the full moon
    Step forth upon the hill,
And memories hard to bear at noon,
    By moonlight harder still,

Form in the shadows of the trees,—
    Things that you could not spare
And live, or so you thought, yet these
    All gone, and you still there,

A man no longer what he was,
    Nor yet the thing he'd planned,
The chilly apple from the grass
    Warmed by your living hand—

I think you will have need of tears;
    I think they will not flow;
Supposing in ten thousand years
    Men ache, as they do now.

Lines for a Grave-Stone

Man alive, that mournst thy lot,
Desiring what thou hast not got,
Money, beauty, love, what not;

Deeming it blesseder to be
A rotted man, than live to see
So rude a sky as covers thee;

Deeming thyself of all unblest
And wretched souls the wretchedest,
Longing to die and be at rest;

Know: that however grim the fate
Which sent thee forth to meditate
Upon my enviable state,

Here lieth one who would resign
Gladly his lot, to shoulder thine.
Give me thy coat; get into mine.

How Naked, How Without a Wall

How naked, how without a wall
   Against the wind and the sharp sleet,
He fares at night, who fares at all
   Forth from the stove's heat.

Or if the moon be in the sky,
   Or if the stars, and the late moon
Not rising till an hour goes by,
   And Libra setting soon,

How naked, how without a stitch
   To shut him from the earnest air,
He goes, who by the whispering ditch
   Alone at night will fare.

Nor is it but the rising chill
   From the warm weeds, that strikes him cold;
Nor that the stridulant hedge grows still,
   Like what has breath to hold,

Until his tiny foot go past
   At length, with its enormous sound;
Nor yet his helpless shadow cast
   To any wolf around.

Bare to the moon and her cold rays
  He takes the road, who by and by
Goes bare beneath the moony gaze
  Of his own awful eye.

He sees his motive, like a fox
  Hid in a badger's hole; he sees
His honour, strangled, in a box,
  Her neck lashed to her knees.

The man who ventures forth alone
  When other men are snug within,
Walks on his marrow, not his bone,
  And lacks his outer skin.

The draughty caverns of his breath
  Grow visible, his heart shines through:
Surely a thing which only death
  Can have the right to do.

From *HUNTSMAN,*
WHAT QUARRY?

The Ballad of Chaldon Down

In April, when the yellow whin
Was out of doors, and I within,—
And magpies nested in the thorn
Where not a man of woman born
Might spy upon them, save he be
Content to bide indefinitely
On Chaldon Heath, hung from a pin,
A great man in a small thorn tree—

In April, when, as I have said,
The golden gorse was all in bloom,
And I confinèd to my room,
And there confinèd to my bed,
As sick as mortal man could be,
A lady came from over the sea,
All for to say good-day to me.

All in a green and silver gown,
With half its flounces in her hand,
She came across the windy down,
She came, and pricked the furrowed land
With heels of slippers built for town,
All for to say good-day to me.

The Channel fog was in her hair,
Her cheek was cool with Channel fog;
Pale cowslips from the sloping hedge,
And samphire from the salty ledge,
And the sweet myrtle of the bog

She brought me as I languished there;
But of the blackthorn, the blue sloe,
No branch to lay a body low.

She came to me by ditch and stile,
She came to me through heather and brake,
And many and many a flinty mile
She walked in April for my sake,
All for to say good-day to me.

She came by way of Lulworth Cove,
She came by way of Diffey's Farm;
All in a green and silver frock,
With half its flounces over her arm,
By the Bat's Head at dusk she came,
Where inland from the Channel drove
The fog, and from the Shambles heard
The horn above the hidden rock;

And startled many a wild sea-bird
To fly unseen from Durdle Door
Into the fog; and left the shore,
And found a track without a name
That led to Chaldon, and so came
Over the downs to Chydyok,
All for to say good-day to me.

All for to ask me only this—
As she shook out her skirts to dry,
And laughed, and looked me in the eye,
And gave me two cold hands to kiss:

That I be steadfast, that I lie
And strengthen and forbear to die.
All for to say that I must be
Son of my sires, who lived to see
The gorse in bloom at ninety-three,
All for to say good-day to me.

The Princess Recalls Her One Adventure

Hard is my pillow
Of down from the duck's breast,
Harsh the linen cover;
I cannot rest.

Fall down, my tears,
Upon the fine hem,
Upon the lonely letters
Of my long name;
Drown the sigh of them.

We stood by the lake
And we neither kissed nor spoke;
We heard how the small waves
Lurched and broke,
And chuckled in the rock.

We spoke and turned away.
We never kissed at all.
Fall down, my tears.
I wish that you might fall

On the road by the lake,
Where my cob went lame,
And I stood with the groom
Till the carriage came.

Short Story

In a fine country, in a sunny country,
Among the hills I knew,
I built a house for the wren that lives in the orchard,
And a house for you.

The house I built for the wren had a round entrance,
Neat and very small;
But the house I built for you had a great doorway,
For a lady proud and tall.

You came from a country where the shrubby sweet
    lavender
Lives the mild winter through;
The lavender died each winter in the garden
Of the house I built for you.

You were troubled and came to me because the farmer
Called the autumn "the fall";
You thought that a country where the lavender died
    in the winter
Was not a country at all.

The wrens return each year to the house in the or-
    chard;

They have lived, they have seen the world, they know
    what's best
For a wren and his wife; in the handsome house I
    gave them
They build their twiggy nest.

But you, you foolish girl, you have gone home
To a leaky castle across the sea,—
To lie awake in linen smelling of lavender,
And hear the nightingale, and long for me.

Pretty Love, I Must Outlive You

Pretty Love, I must outlive you;
And my little dog Llewelyn,
Dreaming here with treble whimpers,
Jerking paws and twitching nostrils
On the hearth-rug, will outlive you,
If no trap or shot-gun gets him.

Parrots, tortoises and redwoods
Live a longer life than men do,
Men a longer life than dogs do,
Dogs a longer life than love does.

What a fool I was to take you,
Pretty Love, into my household,
Shape my days and nights to charm you,
Center all my hopes about you,
Knowing well I must outlive you,
If no trap or shot-gun gets me.

English Sparrows

(Washington Square)

How sweet the sound in the city an hour before sun-
    rise,
When the park is empty and grey and the light clear
    and so lovely
I must sit on the floor before my open window for an
    hour with my arms on the sill
And my cheek on my arm, watching the spring sky's
Soft suffusion from the roofed horizon upward with
    palest rose,
Doting on the charming sight with eyes
Open, eyes closed;
Breathing with quiet pleasure the cool air cleansed by
    the night, lacking all will
To let such happiness go, nor thinking the least thing
    ill
In me for such indulgence, pleased with the day and
    with myself. How sweet
The noisy chirping of the urchin sparrows from crevice
    and shelf
Under my window, and from down there in the
    street,
Announcing the advance of the roaring competitive
    day with city bird-song.

A bumbling bus
Goes under the arch. A man bareheaded and alone
Walks to a bench and sits down.

He breathes the morning with me; his thoughts are
    his own.
Together we watch the first magnanimous
Rays of the sun on the tops of greening trees and on
    houses of red brick and of stone.

Impression: Fog Off the Coast of Dorset

As day was born, as night was dying,
The seagulls woke me with their crying;
And from the reef the mooing horn
Spoke to the waker: Day is born
And night is dying, but still the fog
On dimly looming deck and spar
Is dewy, and on the vessel's log,
And cold the first-mate's fingers are,
And wet the pen wherewith they write
"Off Portland. Fog. No land in sight."
—As night was dying, and glad to die,
And day, with dull and gloomy eye,
Lifting the sun, a smoky lamp,
Peered into fog, that swaddled sky
And wave alike: a shifty damp
Unwieldy province, loosely ruled,
Turned over to a prince unschooled,
That he must govern with sure hand
Straightway, not knowing sea from land.

The Rabbit

Hearing the hawk squeal in the high sky
I and the rabbit trembled.
Only the dark small rabbits newly kittled in their
    neatly dissembled
Hollowed nest in the thicket thatched with straw
Did not respect his cry.
At least, not that I saw.

But I have said to the rabbit with rage and a hundred
    times, "Hop!
Streak it for the bushes! Why do you sit so still?
You are bigger than a house, I tell you, you are
    bigger than a hill, you are a beacon for air-
    planes!
O indiscreet!
And the hawk and all my friends are out to kill!
Get under cover!" But the rabbit never stirred; she
    never will.

And I shall see again and again the large eye blaze
With death, and gently glaze;
The leap into the air I shall see again and again, and
    the kicking feet;
And the sudden quiet everlasting, and the blade of
    grass green in the strange mouth of the inter-
    rupted grazer.

Song for Young Lovers in a City

Though less for love than for the deep
Though transient death that follows it
These childish mouths grown soft in sleep
Here in a rented bed have met,

They have not met in love's despite . . .
Such tiny loves will leap and flare
Lurid as coke-fires in the night,
Against a background of despair.

To treeless grove, to grey retreat
Descend in flocks from corniced eaves
The pigeons now on sooty feet,
To cover them with linden leaves.

To a Calvinist in Bali

You that are sprung of northern stock,
And nothing lavish,—born and bred
With tablets at your foot and head,
And CULPA carven in the rock,

Sense with delight but not with ease
The fragrance of the quinine trees,
The *kembang-spatu's* lolling flame
With solemn envy kin to shame.

Ah, be content!—the scorpion's tail
Atones for much; without avail
Under the sizzling solar pan
Our sleeping servant pulls the fan.

Even in this island richly blest,
Where Beauty walks with naked breast,
Earth is too harsh for Heaven to be
One little hour in jeopardy.

Thanksgiving Dinner

Ah, broken garden, frost on the melons and on the
    beans!
Frozen are the ripe tomatoes, the red fruit and the
    hairy golden stem;
Frozen are the grapes, and the vine above them frozen,
    and the peppers are frozen!
And I walk among them smiling,—for what of them?

I can live on the woody fibres of the overgrown
Kohl-rabi, on the spongy radish coarse and hot,
I can live on what the squirrels may have left of the
    beechnuts and the acorns . . .
For pride in my love, who might well have died, and
    did not.

I will cook for my love a banquet of beets and cab-
    bages,
Leeks, potatoes, turnips, all such fruits . . .
For my clever love, who has returned from further
    than the far east;
We will laugh like spring above the steaming, stolid
    winter roots.

The Snow Storm

No hawk hangs over in this air:
The urgent snow is everywhere.
The wing adroiter than a sail
Must lean away from such a gale,
Abandoning its straight intent,
Or else expose tough ligament
And tender flesh to what before
Meant dampened feathers, nothing more.

Forceless upon our backs there fall
Infrequent flakes hexagonal,
Devised in many a curious style
To charm our safety for a while,
Where close to earth like mice we go
Under the horizontal snow.

Huntsman, What Quarry?

"Huntsman, what quarry
On the dry hill
Do your hounds harry?

When the red oak is bare
And the white oak still
Rattles its leaves
In the cold air:
What fox runs there?"

"Girl, gathering acorns
In the cold autumn,
I hunt the hot pads
That ever run before,
I hunt the pointed mask
That makes no reply,
I hunt the red brush
Of remembered joy."

"To tame or to destroy?"

"To destroy."

"Huntsman, hard by
In a wood of grey beeches
Whose leaves are on the ground,
Is a house with a fire;
You can see the smoke from here.
There's supper and a soft bed

And not a soul around.
Come with me there;
Bide there with me;
And let the fox run free."

The horse that he rode on
Reached down its neck,
Blew upon the acorns,
Nuzzled them aside;
The sun was near setting;
He thought, "Shall I heed her?"
He thought, "Shall I take her
For a one-night's bride?"

He smelled the sweet smoke,
He looked the lady over;
Her hand was on his knee;
But like a flame from cover
The red fox broke—
And "Hoick! Hoick!" cried he.

Not So Far as the Forest

I

That chill is in the air
Which the wise know well, and even have learned to
    bear.
This joy, I know,
Will soon be under snow.

The sun sets in a cloud
And is not seen.
Beauty, that spoke aloud,
Addresses now only the remembering ear.
The heart begins here
To feed on what has been.

Night falls fast.
Today is in the past.

Blown from the dark hill hither to my door
Three flakes, then four
Arrive, then many more.

II

Branch by branch
This tree has died. Green only
Is one last bough, moving its leaves in the sun.

What evil ate its root, what blight,
What ugly thing,
Let the mole say, the bird sing;
Or the white worm behind the shedding bark
Tick in the dark.

You and I have only one thing to do:
Saw the trunk through.

III

Distressèd mind, forbear
To tease the hooded Why;
That shape will not reply.

From the warm chair
To the wind's welter
Flee, if storm's your shelter.

But no, you needs must part,
Fling him his release—
On whose ungenerous heart
Alone you are at peace.

IV

Not dead of wounds, not borne
Home to the village on a litter of branches, torn
By splendid claws and the talk all night of the
    villagers,
But stung to death by gnats
Lies Love.

What swamp I sweated through for all these years
Is at length plain to me.

V

Poor passionate thing,
Even with this clipped wing how well you flew!—
    though not so far as the forest.

Unwounded and unspent, serene but for the eye's
    bright trouble,
Was it the lurching flight, the unequal wind under the
    lopped feathers that brought you down,
To sit in folded colours on the level empty field,
Visible as a ship, paling the yellow stubble?

Rebellious bird, warm body foreign and bright,
Has no one told you?—Hopeless is your flight
Towards the high branches. Here is your home,
Between the barnyard strewn with grain and the
    forest tree.
Though Time refeather the wing,
Ankle slip the ring,
The once-confined thing
Is never again free.

———————

Rendezvous

Not for these lovely blooms that prank your chambers
    did I come. Indeed,
I could have loved you better in the dark;
That is to say, in rooms less bright with roses, rooms
    more casual, less aware
Of History in the wings about to enter with benevolent
    air
On ponderous tiptoe, at the cue "Proceed."
Not that I like the ash-trays over-crowded and the
    place in a mess,
Or the monastic cubicle too unctuously austere and
    stark,
But partly that these formal garlands for our Eighth
    Street Aphrodite are a bit too Greek,
And partly that to make the poor walls rich with our
    unaided loveliness
Would have been more *chic*.

Yet here I am, having told you of my quarrel with the
    taxi-driver over a line of Milton, and you laugh;
    and you are you, none other.
Your laughter pelts my skin with small delicious
    blows.
But I am perverse: I wish you had not scrubbed—with
    pumice, I suppose—
The tobacco stains from your beautiful fingers. And I
    wish I did not feel like your mother.

The Fitting

The fitter said, "*Madame, vous avez maigri,*"
And pinched together a handful of skirt at my hip.
"*Tant mieux,*" I said, and looked away slowly, and
    took my under-lip
Softly between my teeth.

               Rip—rip!
Out came the seam, and was pinned together in an-
    other place.
She knelt before me, a hardworking woman with a
    familiar and unknown face,
Dressed in linty black, very tight in the arm's-eye and
    smelling of sweat.
She rose, lifting my arm, and set her cold shears against
    me,—snip-snip;
Her knuckles gouged my breast. My drooped eyes lifted
    to my guarded eyes in the glass, and glanced away
    as from someone they had never met.

"*Ah, que madame a maigri!*" cried the *vendeuse,*
    coming in with dresses over her arm.
"*C'est la chaleur,*" I said, looking out into the sunny
    tops of the horse-chestnuts—and indeed it was very
    warm.

I stood for a long time so, looking out into the after-
    noon, thinking of the evening and you. . . .

While they murmured busily in the distance, turning
    me, touching my secret body, doing what they
    were paid to do.

What Savage Blossom

Do I not know what savage blossom only under the
    pitting hail
Of your inclement climate could have prospered? Here
    lie
Green leaves to wade in, and of the many roads not
    one road leading outward from this place
But is blocked by boughs that will hiss and simmer
    when they burn—green autumn, lady, green
    autumn on this land!

Do I not know what inward pressure only could inflate
    its petals to withstand
(No, no, not hate, not hate) the onslaught of a little
    time with you?

No, no, not love, not love. Call it by name,
Now that it's over, now that it is gone and cannot hear
    us.

It was an honest thing. Not noble. Yet no shame.

Menses

(He speaks, but to himself, being aware how it is with her)

Think not I have not heard.
Well-fanged the double word
And well-directed flew.

I felt it. Down my side
Innocent as oil I see the ugly venom slide:
Poison enough to stiffen us both, and all our friends;
But I am not pierced, so there the mischief ends.

There is more to be said; I see it coiling;
The impact will be pain.
Yet coil; yet strike again.
You cannot riddle the stout mail I wove
Long since, of wit and love.

As for my answer . . . stupid in the sun
He lies, his fangs drawn:
I will not war with you.

You know how wild you are. You are willing to be
    turned
To other matters; you would be grateful, even.
You watch me shyly. I (for I have learned
More things than one in our few years together)
Chafe at the churlish wind, the unseasonable
    weather.

"Unseasonable?" you cry, with harsher scorn
Than the theme warrants; "Every year it is the same!
'Unseasonable!' they whine, these stupid peasants!—
    and never since they were born
Have they known a spring less wintry! Lord, the
    shame,
The crying shame of seeing a man no wiser than the
    beasts he feeds—
His skull as empty as a shell!"

("Go to. You are unwell.")

Such is my thought, but such are not my words.

"What is the name," I ask, "of those big birds
With yellow breast and low and heavy flight,
That make such mournful whistling?"

                                    "Meadowlarks,"
You answer primly, not a little cheered.
"Some people shoot them." Suddenly your eyes are
    wet
And your chin trembles. On my breast you lean,
And sob most pitifully for all the lovely things that
    are not and have been.

"How silly I am!—and I *know* how silly I am!"
You say; "You are very patient. You are very kind.
I shall be better soon. Just Heaven consign and damn
To tedious Hell this body with its muddy feet in my
    mind!"

The Plaid Dress

Strong sun, that bleach
The curtains of my room, can you not render
Colourless this dress I wear?—
This violent plaid
Of purple angers and red shames; the yellow stripe
Of thin but valid treacheries; the flashy green of kind
    deeds done
Through indolence, high judgments given in haste;
The recurring checker of the serious breach of taste?

No more uncoloured than unmade,
I fear, can be this garment that I may not doff;
Confession does not strip it off,
To send me homeward eased and bare;

All through the formal, unoffending evening, under
    the clean
Bright hair,
Lining the subtle gown . . . it is not seen,
But it is there.

"Fontaine, Je Ne Boirai Pas De Ton Eau!"

I know I might have lived in such a way
As to have suffered only pain:
Loving not man nor dog;
Not money, even; feeling
Toothache perhaps, but never more than an hour
    away
From skill and novocaine;
Making no contacts, dealing with life through agents,
    drinking one cocktail, betting two dollars, wear-
    ing raincoats in the rain;
Betrayed at length by no one but the fog
Whispering to the wing of the plane.

"Fountain," I have cried to that unbubbling well, "I
    will not drink of thy water!" Yet I thirst
For a mouthful of—not to swallow, only to rinse my
    mouth in—peace. And while the eyes of the past
    condemn,
The eyes of the present narrow into assignation. And
    . . . worst . . .
The young are so old, they are born with their fingers
    crossed; I shall get no help from them.

Intention to Escape from Him

I think I will learn some beautiful language, useless
    for commercial
Purposes, work hard at that.
I think I will learn the Latin name of every song-
    bird, not only in America but wherever they
    sing.
(Shun meditation, though; invite the controversial:
Is the world flat? Do bats eat cats?) By digging hard
    I might deflect that river, my mind, that uncon-
    trollable thing,
Turgid and yellow, strong to overflow its banks in
    spring, carrying away bridges;
A bed of pebbles now, through which there trickles
    one clear narrow stream, following a course hence-
    forth nefast—

Dig, dig; and if I come to ledges, blast.

To a Young Poet

Time cannot break the bird's wing from the bird.
Bird and wing together
Go down, one feather.

No thing that ever flew,
Not the lark, not you,
Can die as others do.

Modern Declaration

I, having loved ever since I was a child a few things,
　　never having wavered
In these affections; never through shyness in the houses
　　of the rich or in the presence of clergymen having
　　denied these loves;
Never when worked upon by cynics like chiropractors
　　having grunted or clicked a vertebra to the dis-
　　credit of these loves;
Never when anxious to land a job having diminished
　　them by a conniving smile; or when befuddled by
　　drink
Jeered at them through heartache or lazily fondled the
　　fingers of their alert enemies; declare

That I shall love you always.
No matter what party is in power;
No matter what temporarily expedient combination of
　　allied interests wins the war;
Shall love you always.

The Road to the Past

It is this that you get for being so far-sighted. Not so
　　many years
For the myopic, as for me,
The delightful shape, implored and hard of heart, pro-
　　ceeding
Into the past unheeding,

(No wave of the hand, no backward look to see
If I still stand there) clear and precise along that road
    appears.

The trees that edge that road run parallel
For eyes like mine past many towns, past hell seen
    plainly;
All that has happened shades that street;
Children all day, even the awkward, the ungainly
Of mind, work out on paper problems more abstruse;
Demonstrably these eyes will close
Before those hedges meet.

The True Encounter

"Wolf!" cried my cunning heart
    At every sheep it spied,
    And roused the countryside.

"Wolf! Wolf!"—and up would start
    Good neighbours, bringing spade
    And pitchfork to my aid.

At length my cry was known:
    Therein lay my release.
I met the wolf alone
    And was devoured in peace.

Theme and Variations

Not even my pride will suffer much;
Not even my pride at all, maybe,
If this ill-timed, intemperate clutch
Be loosed by you and not by me,
Will suffer; I have been so true
A vestal to that only pride
Wet wood cannot extinguish, nor
Sand, nor its embers scattered, for,
See all these years, it has not died.

And if indeed, as I dare think,
You cannot push this patient flame,
By any breath your lungs could store,
Even for a moment to the floor
To crawl there, even for a moment crawl,
What can you mix for me to drink
That shall deflect me? What you do
Is either malice, crude defense
Of ego, or indifference:
I know these things as well as you;
You do not dazzle me at all.

Some love, and some simplicity,
Might well have been the death of me.

Heart, do not bruise the breast
That sheltered you so long;
Beat quietly, strange guest.

Or have I done you wrong
To feed you life so fast?
Why, no; digest this food
And thrive. You could outlast
Discomfort if you would.

You do not know for whom
These tears drip through my hands.
You thud in the bright room
Darkly. This pain demands
No action on your part,
Who never saw that face.

These eyes, that let him in,
(Not you, my guiltless heart)
These eyes, let them erase
His image, blot him out
With weeping, and go blind.

Heart, do not stain my skin
With bruises; go about
Your simple function. Mind,
Sleep now; do not intrude;
And do not spy; be kind.

Sweet blindness, now begin.

Rolled in the trough of thick desire,
No oars, and no sea-anchor out
To bring my bow into the pyre
Of sunset, suddenly chilling out
To shadow over sky and sea,
And the boat helpless in the trough;
No oil to pour; no power in me
To breast these waves, to shake them off:

I feel such pity for the poor,
Who take the fracas on the beam—
Being ill-equipped, being insecure—
Daily; and caulk the opening seam
With strips of shirt and scribbled rhyme;
Who bail disaster from the boat
With a pint can; and have no time,
Being so engrossed to keep afloat,
Even for quarrelling (that chagrined
And lavish comfort of the heart),
Who never came into the wind,
Who took life beam-on from the start.

IV

And do you think that love itself,
Living in such an ugly house,
Can prosper long?

                  We meet and part;
Our talk is all of heres and nows,
Our conduct likewise; in no act
Is any future, any past;
Under our sly, unspoken pact,
I know with whom I saw you last,
But I say nothing; and you know
At six-fifteen to whom I go.

Can even love be treated so?

I know, but I do not insist,
Having stealth and tact, though not enough,
What hour your eye is on your wrist.
No wild appeal, no mild rebuff
Deflates the hour, leaves the wine flat.

Yet if you drop the picked-up book
To intercept my clockward look—
Tell me, can love go on like that?

Even the bored, insulted heart,
That signed so long and tight a lease,
Can break its contract, slump in peace.

V

I had not thought so tame a thing
Could deal me this bold suffering.

I have loved badly, loved the great
Too soon, withdrawn my words too late;
And eaten in an echoing hall
Alone and from a chipped plate
The words that I withdrew too late.
Yet even so, when I recall
How ardently, ah! and to whom
Such praise was given, I am not sad:
The very rafters of this room
Are honoured by the guests it had.

You only, being unworthy quite
And specious,—never, as I think,
Having noticed how the gentry drink
Their poison, how administer
Silence to those they would inter—
Have brought me to dementia's brink.
Not that this blow be dealt to *me:*
But by thick hands, and clumsily.

VI

Leap now into this quiet grave.
How cool it is. Can you endure
Packed men and their hot rivalries—
The plodding rich, the shiftless poor,
The bold inept, the weak secure—
Having smelt this grave, how cool it is?

Why, here's a house, why, here's a bed
For every lust that drops its head
In sleep, for vengeance gone to seed,
For the slashed vein that will not bleed,
The jibe unheard, the whip unfelt,
The mind confused, the smooth pelt
Of the breast, compassionate and brave.
Pour them into this quiet grave.

VII

Now from a stout and more imperious day
Let dead impatience arm me for the act.
We bear too much. Let the proud past gainsay
This tolerance. Now, upon the sleepy pact
That bound us two as lovers, now in the night
And ebb of love, let me with stealth proceed,
Catch the vow nodding, harden, feel no fright,
Bring forth the weapon sleekly, do the deed.

I know—and having seen, shall not deny—
This flag inverted keeps its colour still;
This moon in wane and scooped against the sky
Blazes in stern reproach. Stare back, my Will—
We can out-gaze it; can do better yet:
We can expunge it. I will not watch it set.

VIII

The time of year ennobles you.
The death of autumn draws you in.

The death of those delights I drew
From such a cramped and troubled source
Ennobles all, including you,
Involves you as a matter of course.

You are not, you have never been
(Nor did I ever hold you such),
Between your banks, that all but touch,
Fit subject for heroic song. . . .
The busy stream not over-strong,
The flood that any leaf could dam. . . .

Yet more than half of all I am
Lies drowned in shallow water here:
And you assume the time of year.

I do not say this love will last;
Yet Time's perverse, eccentric power
Has bound the hound and stag so fast
That strange companions mount the tower
Where Lockhart's fate with Keats' is cast,
And Booth with Lincoln shares the hour.

That which has quelled me, lives with me,
Accomplice in catastrophe.

Inert Perfection

"Inert Perfection, let me chip your shell.
You cannot break it through with that soft beak.
What if you broke it never, and it befell
You should not issue thence, should never speak?"

Perfection in the egg, a fluid thing,
Grows solid in due course, and there exists;
Knowing no urge to struggle forth and sing;
Complete, though shell-bound. But the mind insists

It shall be hatched . . . to this ulterior end:
That it be bound by Function, that it be
Less than Perfection, having to expend
Some force on a nostalgia to be free.

Czecho-Slovakia

If there were balm in Gilead, I would go
To Gilead for your wounds, unhappy land,
Gather you balsam there, and with this hand,
Made deft by pity, cleanse and bind and sew
And drench with healing, that your strength might
     grow,
(Though love be outlawed, kindness contraband)
And you, O proud and felled, again might stand;
But where to look for balm, I do not know.
The oils and herbs of mercy are so few;
Honour's for sale; allegiance has its price;
The barking of a fox has bought us all;
We save our skins a craven hour or two.—
While Peter warms him in the servants' hall
The thorns are platted and the cock crows twice.

Say that We Saw Spain Die

Say that we saw Spain die. O splendid bull, how well
     you fought!
Lost from the first.

                    . . . the tossed, the replaced, the
     watchful *torero* with gesture elegant and spry,

Before the dark, the tiring but the unglazed eye de-
ploying the bright cape,
Which hid for once not air, but the enemy indeed, the
authentic shape,
A thousand of him, interminably into the ring re-
leased . . . the turning beast at length between
converging colours caught.

Save for the weapons of its skull, a bull
Unarmed, considering, weighing, charging
Almost a world, itself without ally.

Say that we saw the shoulders more than the mind
confused, so profusely
Bleeding from so many more than the accustomed
barbs, the game gone vulgar, the rules abused.

Say that we saw Spain die from loss of blood, a rustic
reason, in a reinforced
And proud punctilious land, no *espada*—
A hundred men unhorsed,
A hundred horses gored, and the afternoon aging, and
the crowd growing restless (all, all so much later
than planned),
And the big head heavy, sliding forward in the sand,
and the tongue dry with sand,—no *espada*
Toward that hot neck, for the delicate and final thrust,
having dared thrust forth his hand.

Set the foot down with distrust upon the crust of the
    world—it is thin.
Moles are at work beneath us; they have tunnelled the
    sub-soil
With separate chambers; which at an appointed
    knock
Could be as one, could intersect and interlock. We
    walk on the skin
Of life. No toil
Of rake or hoe, no lime, no phosphate, no rotation of
    crops, no irrigation of the land,
Will coax the limp and flattened grain to stand
On that bad day, or feed to strength the nibbled roots
    of our nation.

Ease has demoralized us, nearly so; we know
Nothing of the rigours of winter: the house has a roof
    against—the car a top against—the snow.
All will be well, we say; it is a habit, like the rising
    of the sun,
For our country to prosper; who can prevail against
    us? No one.

The house has a roof; but the boards of its floor are
    rotting, and hall upon hall
The moles have built their palace beneath us: we
    have not far to fall.

Three Sonnets in Tetrameter

I

See how these masses mill and swarm
And troop and muster and assail:
God!—We could keep this planet warm
By friction, if the sun should fail.
Mercury, Saturn, Venus, Mars:
If no prow cuts your arid seas,
Then in your weightless air no wars
Explode with such catastrophes
As rock our planet all but loose
From its frayed mooring to the sun.
Law will not sanction such abuse
Forever; when the mischief's done,
Planets, rejoice, on which at night
Rains but the twelve-ton meteorite.

II

His stalk the dark delphinium
Unthorned into the tending hand
Releases . . . yet that hour will come . . .
And must, in such a spiny land.
The silky, powdery mignonette
Before these gathering dews are gone
May pierce me—does the rose regret
The day she did her armour on?

In that the foul supplants the fair,
The coarse defeats the twice-refined,
Is food for thought, but not despair:
All will be easier when the mind
To meet the brutal age has grown
An iron cortex of its own.

III

No further from me than my hand
Is China that I loved so well;
Love does not help to understand
The logic of the bursting shell.
Perfect in dream above me yet
Shines the white cone of Fuji-San;
I wake in fear, and weep and sweat . . .
Weep for Yoshida, for Japan.
Logic alone, all love laid by,
Must calm this crazed and plunging star:
Sorrowful news for such as I,
Who hoped—with men just as they are,
Sinful and loving—to secure
A human peace that might endure.

Two Voices

FIRST VOICE

Let us be circumspect, surrounded as we are
By every foe but one, and he from the woods
    watching.
Let us be courteous, since we cannot be wise, guilty
    of no neglect, pallid with seemly terror, yet re-
    garding with indulgent eyes
Violence, and compromise.

SECOND VOICE

We shall learn nothing; or we shall learn it too late.
    Why should we wait
For Death, who knows the road so well? Need we sit
    hatching—
Such quiet fowl as we, meek to the touch,—a clutch of
    adder's eggs? Let us not turn them; let us not
    keep them warm; let us leave our nests and flock
    and tell
All that we know, all that we can piece together, of a
    time when all went, or seemed to go, well.

Mortal Flesh, Is Not Your Place
in the Ground?

Mortal flesh, is not your place in the ground?—Why
    do you stare so
At the bright planet serene in the clear green eve-
    ning sky above the many-coloured streakèd
    clouds?—
Your brows drawn together as if to chide, your mouth
    set as if in anger.

Learn to love blackness while there is yet time,
    blackness
Unpatterned, blackness without horizons.

Beautiful are the trees in autumn, the emerald pines
Dark among the light-red leaves of the maple and the
    dark-red
Leaves of the white oak and the indigo long
Leaves of the white ash.
But why do you stand so, staring with stern face of
    ecstasy at the autumn leaves,
At the boughs hung with banners along the road as if
    a procession were about to pass?

Learn to love roots instead, that soon above your head
    shall be as branches.

No Earthly Enterprise

No earthly enterprise
Will cloud this vision; so beware,
You whom I love, when you are weak, of seeking com-
    fort stair by stair
Up here: which leads nowhere.

I am at home—oh, I am safe in bed and well tucked in
    —Despair
Put out the light beside my bed.
I smiled, and closed my eyes.
"Goodnight—goodnight," she said.

But you, you do not like this frosty air.

Cold of the sun's eclipse,
When cocks crow for the first time hopeless, and dogs
    in kennel howl,
Abandoning the richly-stinking bone,
And the star at the edge of the shamed and altered
    sun shivers alone,
And over the pond the bat but not the swallow dips,
And out comes the owl.

Lines Written in Recapitulation

I could not bring this splendid world nor any trading
    beast
In charge of it, to defer, no, not to give ear, not in the
    least
Appearance, to my handsome prophecies, which here
    I ponder and put by.

I am left simpler, less encumbered, by the con-
    sciousness that I shall by no pebble in my dirty
    sling avail
To slay one purple giant four feet high and distribute
    arms among his tall attendants, who spit at his
    name when spitting on the ground:
They will be found one day
Prone where they fell, or dead sitting—and a pock-
    marked wall
Supporting the beautiful back straight as an oak be-
    fore it is old.

I have learned to fail. And I have had my say.
Yet shall I sing until my voice crack (this being my
    leisure, this my holiday)
That man was a special thing and no commodity, a
    thing improper to be sold.

This Dusky Faith

Why, then, weep not,
Since naught's to weep.

Too wild, too hot
For a dead thing,
Altered and cold,
Are these long tears:
Relinquishing
To the sovereign force
Of the pulling past
What you cannot hold
Is reason's course.

Wherefore, sleep.

Or sleep to the rocking
Rather, of this:
The silver knocking
Of the moon's knuckles
At the door of the night;
Death here becomes
Being, nor truckles
To the sun, assumes
Light as its right.

So, too, this dusky faith
In Man, transcends its death,
Shines out, gains emphasis;
Shorn of the tangled past,
Shows its fine skill at last,
Cold, lovely satellite.

Truce for a Moment

Truce for a moment between Earth and Ether
Slackens the mind's allegiance to despair:
Shyly confer earth, water, fire and air
With the fifth essence.

For the duration, if the mind require it,
Trigged is the wheel of Time against the slope;
Infinite Space lies curved within the scope
Of the hand's cradle.

Thus between day and evening in the autumn,
High in the west alone and burning bright,
Venus has hung, the earliest riding-light
In the calm harbour.

INDEX TO FIRST LINES